JESUS

Is Coming Back...

SOON

Bishop Eric A. Lambert Jr.

ISBN 978-1-63903-849-7 (paperback)
ISBN 978-1-63903-850-3 (digital)

Christian Faith Publishing, Inc.
832 Park Avenue
Meadville, PA 16335
www.christianfaithpublishing.com

Printed in the United States of America

PROLOGUE

The vast swirling clouds that encompassed them allowed the group to move forward in small steps. Although they could not see more than a few feet ahead, they were very peaceful. A moment ago, they heard the trumpet blast, and the following words they heard were as clear as the sound of a bell: "Jesus is here, go to meet Him!"

The next thing the group noticed was beautiful. These people were in the atmospheric heaven. Then as rapidly as that happened, they were among the planets. The next sight was breathtaking. The people were in the city of heaven and seeing loved ones who had gone before. They saw the beauty of heaven, and there was a reunion with the family of God.

The air was sweet-smelling, and there was no feeling of dread or darkness. In fact, all of the people felt a sense of love mixed with joy and peace. There was laughter such as the people had never heard; it was not frustrating laughter but pure laughter, which affected the surroundings.

As they walked further into the city, giant angels were walking and flying around. Each seemed to be on a mission, and they were not to be hindered. The singing was absolutely fabulous, and the words all reflected the glory of the Lord Jesus. What caught the attention of these newcomers was the absence of darkness, and there were no shadows. The people were happy, for they had been caught up to meet the Lord, and they were in heaven. Now the one question on their mind was spoken in unison: "Where was Jesus?" They just had to say thank you to the Lamb of God for dying for them and bringing them to this beautiful, glorious place. However, while these people were walking in the glory of God, things on earth were getting worse. Unfortunately, many were not ready for this beautiful place.

CHAPTER 1

As the workday faded to a close, Philip Bullock glanced at his watch. He had been in the office since seven that morning, and he was mentally and physically drained. Philip had worked as a research biologist at Jones Pharmaceuticals for twenty years. As the leader of a team of biologists, the work had become mentally fatiguing. Philip cleared his desk as colleagues Bill and Tom stopped by his office door.

"Long day," Bill said, shaking his head. "Want to go out for a few drinks?"

"Thanks, but no," Philip politely declined, powering down his computer.

Tom saluted playfully as the two continued down the corridor toward the exit.

Pausing to reflect on whether his colleagues thought him unsociable, Philip thought, *After all, I gave my life to Jesus Christ, which changes who I am and my relationship to God. I cannot allow my flesh to ruin this tremendous gift.*

Taking his jacket from the coat rack, Philip paused for another look at the framed family photo sitting on the credenza. His heart warmed as he looked at Linda, his wife of thirty-five years, standing beside him, both wearing casual summer outfits. Next to his wife stood Ricky. He was the oldest son, with more of a grimace than a smile on his face. Marie, their daughter, was beside Ricky, and Nicolas, the baby boy, stood at Philip's right elbow.

"Thank you, God, for such a fine family," Philip whispered as he stood before the picture. As his gaze moved toward the eldest

5

child, he added, "Lord, please bring Ricky to the cross and help him find his way to Jesus. I feel urgently you are returning soon, and I want my son with our family in heaven."

Philip Bullock came from a long family line of day laborers. His father had been a long-distance truck driver for a national retail chain, and his grandfather had worked in the Pennsylvania steel mills. Family lore revealed that his great-grandfather had been the son of freed slaves. *Never again* became the family motto upheld by his descendants. The Bullocks would serve no master in the future.

Coming of age in the late twentieth century, Philip had learned plenty about civil rights and personal freedom and the right to be whatever you want to be; no one could hold you back. A strong man with broad shoulders, possibly stemming from his forebears' hard work, Philip was nevertheless more of a thinking man and courteous by nature. He went to college and earned a biology degree, which is how he could be hired at Jones Pharmaceuticals following graduation. Philip did not have to fight for his rights; he earned them by going to college and paying his academic dues.

At the only fraternity party he attended, more from curiosity than interest, he met Linda, a lovely, well-spoken young lady earning a nursing degree. His biology classes helped him make small talk that night instead of drinking or getting rowdy. Phil and Linda continued seeing each other on campus, and Phil introduced her to his parents when they came to the university to visit.

"She's a nice girl," his mother said warmly after they had all eaten dinner together and dropped Linda off at her dorm. "Not many around like her these days."

"Got a head on her shoulders too," his father John said approvingly as he pulled the Ford Taurus out of the dorm parking lot.

That was all they needed to say. Philip knew them well enough to understand that they approved of Linda. He was glad because he was enjoying spending time with her more and more.

Linda's father had died in a car accident several years before. But her mother came to visit the campus and was introduced to Philip.

"My, you're tall," the petite woman with a curious expression said as she glanced at him.

"I can't help it, ma'am," Philip said to be funny, and the two women smiled.

Over dinner at the Student Union pizzeria, Philip outlined his plans, which at this point were simple: He would graduate the following year and look for a job. Then he hoped to "settle down," a euphemism for "get married," and Mrs. Johnson understood. Having been a critical care nurse for decades, she knew how to read people's expressions and interpret simple phrases into meaningful statements. She liked Phil Bullock and knew her daughter did too.

"Does the campus have a church service on Sundays you all can attend?" she asked politely over a dessert of ice cream sundaes.

"No, ma'am," Philip said after exchanging a glance with Linda. "Your daughter has invited me on several occasions, but my studies take up all my time."

Wiping her mouth, Mrs. Johnson said, "Well, Philip, I encourage you to make time for the Lord. There is no better use for your time. Put him first, and the rest will fall into place. Matthew 6:33, Jesus's own words."

"Yes, ma'am," he said to be polite rather than to agree. His parents had gone to church most of the time. And as a boy, Philip had attended Sunday school and joined the children's choir. But as a teenager, he had drifted away, was involved with his high school football team, and worked on his grades to get into college. Despite occasional reminders, his parents did not try to force him to go to church as he got older. His older sister had gone away to college in New York and married one of her social work classmates, so the family only saw them on holidays. John and Leona Bullock decided to let their son make his own choices about church and faith.

Linda blushed and glanced down at her ice cream, embarrassed her mother had raised the topic but glad she had done so. Faith was important to Linda too, but she did not want to push her beliefs onto Philip.

For the next eighteen months, Phil and Linda dated steadily. In their senior year at Christmas, Phil proposed and gave her an engagement ring while walking in the nearby downtown area decorated with holiday lights. Linda accepted with tears of joy. The pair spent their last semester of college working hard to finish the required courses and apply for professional jobs as well as planning their wedding back in Linda's hometown of Reading. Phil interviewed for Johnson Pharmaceuticals and was hired a week later. Linda got a job as an ob-gyn nurse at a suburban Philadelphia hospital.

"Honey, should I ask Pastor Smith to lead our wedding service?" Linda asked one night as they were studying in the dorm's common area. She was not sure if Phil would like the idea of her pastor giving the service, but he had not mentioned the pastor from his family's church being involved.

"Sure, whatever you want," he looked up from the paper he was typing on the computer and smiled.

"He may want us to take some premarital classes before the wedding," she said cautiously. Fortunately, there were no other students around just then to hear their private conversation.

Staring at the computer monitor in concentration, Phil murmured, "Classes? How many?"

"Oh, probably three or four. Routine stuff," she said casually.

"Well okay, ask him if he can do it on the weekends this summer."

Their wedding was scheduled for August 21, and Pastor Smith agreed to meet with the couple for three Saturdays in July. By their first appointment, graduation parties were behind them, and both Phil and Linda had started their new jobs. It was a bit stressful, but Phil reminded himself that hard work could fix just about anything, and he knew he would adjust. Linda was a little nervous working with women in labor and handling newborns, but her natural strength and eye for detail inherited from her mother helped her acclimate quickly.

The counseling sessions went smoothly for the most part. When Reverend Smith asked about the couple's church plans and spiritual goals, Phil glanced at Linda as if to say, *you can take it from here.* Reverend Smith had counseled more than a few couples, and he had seen this scenario before.

"Just get in the Word daily, son," he advised Phil. "Linda will be depending on you to lead the family, won't you?"

As he glanced at Linda, she looked up in surprise. Being raised by a single mother for several years, Linda knew little about male leadership in the home, but suddenly, it sounded like a good idea. It would take some of the burdens off her to make all the decisions and run family life.

Likewise surprised, Phil said, "Oh, okay. I do not have much experience with spiritual leadership. I've been mostly a follower." He paused, but the reverend waited for him to continue. "All right, I'll read the Bible as much as possible," he said.

"Great," Reverend Smith beamed. "I know you will be a fine family leader."

The summer passed quickly, and soon it was time for the nuptials. Everything had been planned smoothly. Leona had been invited to help Sarah Johnson and Linda manage all the wedding details, along with the assistance of a host of aunts and cousins from both families.

As Phil stood before the altar facing his beloved Linda, her beautiful face and the sanctity of the moment brought tears to his eyes.

Pastor Smith's voice broke into his reverie: "Marriage is a sacred union and a holy gift ordained by God and given to humanity when he created Adam and Eve exclusively for each other. No one and nothing can ever separate us from the love of God, Paul tells us in Romans 8:39. The same should be the standing rule for your marriage: Let nothing or no one come between you. Be united in your love for God and for each other..."

As these words sank into the depths of Philip's soul, his heart was awakened to the spiritual love of God for all humans. He now reflected on how much he and Linda would need the love of God to help them in their new life. God had brought them together forever! He stared into her eyes and found her love for him reflected from her love for their heavenly Father: pure, unadulterated, devoted.

Phil had never experienced this feeling before—not just romantic love but a massive wave of divine love that swept through his soul and removed the doubt and the debris of sin that had collected over his lifetime. He felt wholly clean for the first time in his life. He murmured, "Thank you, God, for loving me and forgiving me. Thank you for Jesus who paid for my sins."

Reverend Smith was still speaking the wedding service and about to ask the vows. Linda saw Philip's lips moving and tears at the corners of his eyes. She could not hear his words, but she could read his face; he had found God!

Tears filled her eyes as she stared at the face of the man she was marrying. Trust and respect overflowed her soul; and silently, she poured out thanks to God.

"Do you, Philip Bullock, take Linda Johnson to be your lawfully wedded wife, to have and to hold…"

"Yes," Philip said firmly with a broad smile as the reverend finished his question.

"Do you, Linda Johnson, take Philip Bullock to be your lawfully wedding husband, to have and to hold…"

"Oh yes, I sure do!" she almost squealed with delight as guests chuckled from the pews.

"Then it is my great pleasure and privilege to pronounce you husband and wife!" Reverend Smith beamed as the newlyweds turned to face the filled church seats. A cheer went up as the couple made their way down the main aisle toward the hall for the reception line. Philip had never been prouder, and Linda had never felt happier. It was the beginning of a dream life together that would one day explode into a nightmare.

Philip settled comfortably into his new job as a research biologist. And thanks to hard work and ethical standards, he was eventually promoted to senior researcher for the company.

"Well look at you," Linda said happily, eyes dancing with merriment, on the afternoon he came home after work, having called to inform her during his lunch break. "I've always wanted to be with a *lead* biologist," she said as she met him at the door with a long kiss that drew Philip's arms tightly around his wife of thirty-five years.

"Great way to start the new millennium." He smiled as they finished the kiss.

Their firstborn son, Ricky, entered the foyer. "Congrats, Dad!" He hugged his father.

Marie darted through the doorway. "Dad, you're amazing! I'm proud of you!"

"Now that's a nice welcome," Philip joked as the others laughed. He looked around and asked, "Where's Nicholas?"

"Up in his room, studying like always," Linda said, linking her arm through her husband's to lead him to the kitchen where a wonderful smell of dinner beckoned.

"Something smells terrific," Philip said. "I'm glad you had today off work. Let me get changed before we eat."

Linda directed Ricky to set the table and carry out the roast beef with mashed potatoes and green beans while Marie filled the drinking glasses with ice water.

Upstairs, Philip paused by his son's room where the door was half-open. "Nicholas? What are you doing, son?"

Nicholas looked up and said, "Hi, Dad! Mom told us about your promotion at work. Congrats!"

Philip smiled at his son's enthusiastic tone. "Thanks. How about you? School okay?"

"Yeah," Nicholas shrugged. "You know how junior year can be, college prep courses and exams."

"I remember," Philip said. "It will pay off when you get accepted to college."

"True," Nicholas said. "I'll be down for dinner in a minute."

As he changed into jogging pants and a T-shirt, Philip paused to pray silently. "Thank you, Lord, for my family and my job promotion. None of this would be possible without you. Please help me guide our family in the right direction, especially Ricky."

When everyone had sat down at the dinner table, Philip said, "I'm grateful for all of you. Our family is what is most important. Each one of us has a role to play, and I will do my best to lead. Let me know if something is bothering you or you need help with anything."

Nicholas raised his hand.

"Yes?" Philip said as Linda began passing the platters of food around the table.

"Thank you for being a great dad."

"Hear, hear," Marie said, tapping her fork on the table.

Ricky said nothing, just glanced at his dad briefly.

They dug in heartily, enjoying the tender, savory roast and fluffy mashed potatoes. The green beans were seasoned lightly with butter and garlic.

"Delicious meal," Philip said, taking a second helping of the beef.

"Yeah, tasty," Ricky said in an almost scornful tone, drawing a sharp glance from his father.

"I'm glad everyone likes it," Linda chirped.

Philip wondered if she was oblivious to their eldest son's sarcasm or deliberately ignoring it. "Church basketball tonight, and I'm coaching," he announced. "You all coming?"

"Count me in," Linda said, "after I load the dishwasher."

"Me too," Nicholas chimed in. "I need the exercise."

Ricky said, "I'm meeting my friends, but maybe we'll drop by."

"I'll be there," Marie said, "but I might have to leave early to study for my math test."

Helping his wife take the dishes to the kitchen, Philip wondered when their family had begun to fracture. They had started off so well when firstborn Ricky came along. Linda had arranged her nursing schedule to spend most days with the newborn while working weekends when Philip could care for the baby. A few years later, they did the same when Nicholas was born. After buying a lovely but not extravagant home in the suburbs, the couple later decided to have their third and last child, Marie.

Right after their wedding, they had joined a church in the Philadelphia community where they settled. Philip kept his word and began reading the Bible most days. Sometimes Linda joined him as one or the other read Scripture aloud, after which they discussed it. As Philip grew in his faith, he was invited to teach a Sunday school class for middle-school kids. He surprised himself by enjoying the class in sharing important Bible messages with the young teens. Years earlier, he had been nominated as a deacon of the church and was voted in by the congregation. Honored by their trust, Philip took the position seriously and joined a men's accountability group to help him stay on the straight and narrow. He did not have a besetting sin or anything like that, but trouble did look his way now and then, and he wanted to be sure and avoid it.

Now going out to the garage to put the sports gear in the car while Linda arranged the dishes in the dishwasher racks and the two younger children got ready, Philip wondered when Ricky took his first wrong turn. Was it in middle school when he got hooked up with some local kids using drugs? Was it in high school when Ricky got expelled for being a gang member—something his parents knew nothing about? Philip and Linda had tried family counseling, quality time, shared hobbies, and enforced volunteerism to guide their son back to a straight path. But somehow, the boy kept wandering off on his own into the dark alleys of Satan's temptations.

Shaking off the negative thoughts, Philip smiled as Linda met him at the door, ready to get into the car with Nicholas and Marie behind her. They would have a good time at the church tonight, like so many others they had enjoyed as a family. But Philip was concerned about his oldest son.

Philip and Linda sat in the fourth pew from the front, their regular seats were due to Philip's deacon status and duties with the other deacons to distribute the service programs and collect the offering. The couple's marriage had grown even stronger, and their children were pretty much adults at this point. But things had not turned out exactly as planned.

As Reverend Abel Skinner began his sermon on the book of 1 Peter, Philip leaned back to relax and absorb the message. But his thoughts refused to settle down as he thought about last night's confrontation with Ricky, now twenty-five, who had come home at 2:00 a.m., clearly under the influence of something illegal. Nicholas had been downstairs playing video games and had heard his brother unlock the front door. He tried helping Ricky up the steps to the bedroom, but the young man stumbled, awakening his parents.

"What do you mean coming home in that condition?" Philip demanded from the top of the stairs as Linda stood beside him, eyes round in dismay at the sight of their disheveled son.

"I'ma…no, there's nuttin' wrong wi' me. It's you…both you…" Ricky struggled for words as his eyes blazed. "You made me do that church crap…" His voice trailed off in a string of profanities.

"Get to bed," Nicholas said sternly, giving his brother a nudge up the steps. At twenty-one, Nicholas was finishing Bible college a year early with plans to go into ministry. Ricky loathed him for that.

Phil started to yell at Ricky and then caught himself as Linda gripped his arm. It would not do any good. Watching to see if Ricky made it to his room, where he slammed the door shut, Philip glanced at Nicholas with relief. "Thank you."

Now, Sunday morning in church, listening to Reverend Skinner talk about the suffering in this world, Philip finally knew what he meant. All his life, Philip had enjoyed a stable and relatively normal upbringing, education, and marriage. Family life had been good until Ricky had reached his teen years and rebelled in full force. It was as if something, or someone, was pulling his strings to make him act out against everything he had been raised with, especially faith and family. Philip and Linda had read books and watched videos, but nothing seemed to help. In fact, Ricky was getting worse.

Philip's pager dinged in his pocket. Pulling it out, he read the monitor message and leaned over to Linda. "We have to leave now."

As Reverend Skinner closed the service in prayer, Phil and Linda got up quietly and left the sanctuary by the side door. As they rushed to their parked car, Linda asked, "What's wrong?"

"Ricky overdosed," Phil said, his blood pressure rising. "We have to get to the ER."

CHAPTER 2

Philip paced nervously in the waiting room as Linda talked to the ER receptionist. Ricky was being evaluated by the doctors, and a toxicology lab report was being processed. The only other person sitting on the far side of the room was an elderly woman who appeared to be waiting for an update about a family member.

A moment later, Linda returned just as Nicholas rushed through the ER door.

"He's stable," she exhaled as if she had been holding her breath. "He's going to be okay."

"What happened?" Nicholas asked, looking from one parent to the other. "I got your text message, and Pastor Skinner dropped me off here."

"Your brother overdosed," Philip said evenly, trying to control the emotions raging inside. "We don't know what he was taking, but you saw him last night. He was on something. Thanks to that no-good gang he runs with."

Linda hugged Nicholas without a word. He always seemed to understand without detailed explanations.

"Do either of you want some coffee or hot chocolate?" Nicholas asked, gesturing toward the machine in the corner.

Neither did. The three sat down on hard vinyl-padded chairs to wait.

Linda finally said, "I don't know what makes Ricky act that way. We raised him better than that. We've shown him love and attention and…"

"It doesn't work with that kind," Philip cut in, using a sharper tone than usual. "Ricky is stubborn, and he won't listen to anybody except those so-called friends of his. He's not going to stop until it's too late."

"Dad, don't worry. Ricky will come to his senses one of these days. We had a talk a few months ago when he gave me a ride after I got a flat tire. He was trying to get straight then, but he didn't say much about it. I saw his hands were shaky, and he was pale. I suggested in a low-key way that a counselor could help him, but he dismissed the idea." Nicholas shook his head in disappointment.

"We've all tried," Linda said softly. "Ricky knows we love him. But he is on a mission to prove himself. But of what, I don't know. Some kids don't get their full judgment until they reach their midtwenties. In a few years, he may settle down. I sure hope so."

A man wearing a white lab coat and holding a patient chart beckoned from the entryway leading to the ER treatment area.

"Ricky Bullock family?" the doctor called.

They stood up and stepped quickly to follow the doctor down a long hall to where he stepped inside a conference room, waited for the family to enter, and closed the door.

"Please sit down," he suggested, taking a seat as well.

When they did, he said, "My name is Dr. Perry, and I have an update on Ricky."

Everyone looked at the doctor expectantly, and he began to speak. "Ricky's toxicology screen showed several substances in his blood, along with an alcohol level over the legal limit. He seemingly took an accidental overdose of methadone. Do you know if it has been prescribed for him as a painkiller?"

"No," Philip said, then asked Linda, "Did you know anything about his taking painkillers?"

She shook her head no with a surprised expression.

"Well someone gave it to him, or he may have bought it on the street. It was a hefty dose, but he should recover. We're going to keep him overnight for observation and release him tomorrow with the recommendation that he follows up with a substance abuse physician or therapist."

"Thank you," Linda and Phil said at the same time. Nicholas appeared crestfallen.

Dr. Scott got up and held out his hand to shake theirs. "He's a legal adult, so we can't release much further information without his consent. But since his condition was touch-and-go at first, you have a right to know legally in case we needed to put him on a ventilator."

Linda gasped, and Phil put an arm around her shoulders. "Thanks again, Dr. Scott," Phil said as the family filed out of the room and headed toward the lobby exit.

"Did you leave a message for Marie?" Linda asked.

"No, there was no time after I texted Nicholas and then Reverend Skinner. Can you do it now?"

As they headed toward their car in the nearby lot, Linda texted Marie a short message. Immediately, her phone dinged as Marie called in a panic. Linda explained the situation quickly. Phil and Nicholas could hear Marie's upset voice coming through Linda's phone.

"Stupid jerk! I told him to stay away from those guys. They're going to kill him one of these days!" Her prediction was the opposite of her mother's. Phil wondered which would be fulfilled.

The drive home was quiet. By now, it was early evening, and Linda offered to make sandwiches for dinner. Marie called again, and Linda went into the other room to explain what happened and provide more details.

Nicholas cleared the table, and Philip went into the study and sat down in his favorite dark blue recliner. Gazing through the paned window glass beside the chair, he could see a peaceful sun setting over the hill behind the houses in their neighborhood. It was a beautiful, calm Sabbath evening that Philip particularly loved. But tonight, as darkness descended, his heart was cold and empty. He felt whipped, and the workday would begin anew early the following day. Resting his head against the soft corduroy fabric of the cushioned chair, Philip wondered what he had done wrong to have a son like Ricky. He loved the boy, who was now a young man, but like King David in the Bible, his son brought him disillusionment and pain and possibly even danger if he brought drugs home with him. People under the influence often turned violent toward family members; and if a drug deal went wrong, someone could get shot accidentally if gang members came gunning for Ricky.

Closing his eyes, Philip recalled those early days of marriage when he and Linda had learned to accept each other's flaws and shortcomings. They had built a union centered on their Christian faith, and that had made all the difference. Many coworkers and friends had been through one or more divorces, and Phil was grateful that he and Linda had found ways to make their marriage work by remaining committed to God and each other.

There had been trials. Once, Linda had gotten a cancer scare when she found a lump. Together, she and Phil had been forced to face the bleak possibility of her life being cut short. Thankfully, with prayer support from the church members and their friends, Phil believed that had contributed to Linda's recovery, and she had been fine ever since.

Then there had been the near scandal of the female assistant the company had hired to work with Phil. Beautiful and confident, the blonde temptress had tried all her tricks to be alone with Phil and seduce him. She was drawn to powerful men and viewed Philip as a prize-worthy catch and a stepping stone for her career. He had been flattered at first by her attention when Linda was feeling depressed and sharing concerns more with her girlfriends than with him. He had felt helpless like he was letting her down somehow. The truth was he did not know what to say that would comfort his wife. But Sierra at work was glib and witty, making conversations easy and light. She made Phil feel valued and sought-after. They almost kissed one evening after work, after staying late to finish a report that was on a deadline. The supervisor had ordered pizza for everyone, and by eight o'clock, the other department members had finished their part of the report and left. As Philip ran the final totals one more time to double-check their accuracy, Sierra had hovered over his shoulder to watch. He felt her closeness, smelled her perfume, and grew momentarily dizzy. As she bent down closer to study the screen, she brushed his shoulder, and he almost lost all control. Commanding everything within him to pull away, he prayed silently, "Lord, help me to escape!"

Pushing back from the desk, he had abruptly stood up and stepped back, reaching for his jacket on the nearby coat rack.

"All done," he said lightly to compose his shaky voice. "Thanks for staying late. Can you get the lights? My wife is holding dinner for me."

Without directly looking at Sierra, he could sense her irritation, but he didn't care. Eagerly, he left the office and took the stairs instead of the elevator to the main floor, hurrying to his car, whispering, "Thank you, Lord."

At first, he said nothing to Linda, not wanting to upset her. Besides, nothing had happened. But his conscience wouldn't let him rest for the next two days. As they got into bed the third night, he took Linda in his arms and told her about the incident.

"I understand," Linda said, kissing his cheek. "I should've been more patient in explaining my feelings to you about this cancer scare. It was just that I wanted to ignore it at first, and I didn't want to upset you. I was upset enough for both of us." They chuckled at that, and Philip kissed her forehead before they fell asleep.

That was one of the few times that Linda had caused him grief, or actually, her avoidance of the issue caused him more pain than irritation. The only other time she had made him feel uncomfortable was right after Marie's birth. Linda had taken a leave of absence from work for several months to care for their baby, knowing it would be their last, and finances were tight. She mentioned, a couple of times, her disappointment that they wouldn't have much money for Christmas gifts that year, and Linda loved the holidays. She enjoyed giving generous gifts to family members and friends. But that year, there wasn't much in the budget for celebrations.

"I can get a second part-time job," Phil offered one morning while shaving as she brushed her teeth. "I could do tax returns for people we know and earn some extra income."

"No," Linda paused her toothbrush movement. "That would be embarrassing. Besides, you're busy enough with your regular job and the yard work." That was in November when he was still mowing a couple of times a month and raking leaves.

Frustration grew as Phil again felt like a failure. He knew Linda didn't see him that way, but he wished they had more money to enjoy the holidays the way she wanted to.

Linda noticed his expression and grew thoughtful. That night after dinner, as they sat down to watch a television movie after the kids were in bed, she said, "I'm sorry about whining for Christmas money. It's not important. Some of my friends talked about going shopping and putting gifts in layaway, and I felt kind of left out. It was selfish of me. We have so much to be grateful for, especially a loving, hardworking husband and father like you." Reaching over to put her hand on his from her matching recliner, Phil felt instant relief and a renewed appreciation for his wife. She indeed was a Proverbs 31 woman, making do with whatever income he could bring home until she returned to work and establishing a comfortable, charming home that they all enjoyed. It didn't hurt that she was a good cook as well.

Returning to the present in his thoughts, Phil noticed it had gotten dark outside. He thought about turning on the television to watch sports, but none of his favorite teams were playing.

Linda entered the room with two mugs of steaming tea. "Here you go, decaf chamomile," she said, setting the mugs on the coffee table before the two recliners.

"Thanks, honey," Phil said, his face brightening. "What did Marie have to say?"

"Oh, the usual rants about Ricky," Linda said, taking a seat in her chair and picking up the mug to sip tea. "She's worried about him like we are. But we're also concerned about his spiritual condition. I see no signs of salvation, do you?" She took a sip from the mug and set it down.

"No," Phil said heavily. "I wish there were even a glint of hope—a Christian friend, occasional church attendance, evidence that he had opened the Bible that we gave him for his birthday with his name engraved on it. But as far as I can see, there is nothing to suggest that Ricky knows the Lord or wants to." He took a couple of sips of tea and set his mug down again.

"You know," Linda said, "the ladies' Bible study I've been attending is going through the book of Revelation. I know you and I have read it before, but it is hard to understand. This group came up with some great insights using the commentaries."

Thinking for a moment, Phil replied, "Maybe it's time for us to take another look. I feel like the time is getting closer for Jesus to return and rapture the church of believers. Reverend Skinner preached on that topic last year, and I keep seeing the signs foretold in the prophecies."

"Me too," Linda said, nodding. "Every day there are more events in the news that show how close we are to the time of the return of Christ. He said it would be like the days of Noah when no one believed that the ark would be needed and laughed at Noah and his family."

"Right," Phil said. "Jesus also said it would be like the days of Sodom and Gomorrah, and that is clearly happening in today's culture."

"Wow, did you ever imagine we would be living in the end-times to see these things come to pass?" Linda asked.

"I never thought much about it while growing up. But since joining our church and getting into the Bible, it has become increasingly clear that we are almost there."

"Let's take a look," Linda said eagerly, pulling the Bible off the coffee table and turning to the book of Revelation.

Phil listened attentively as she began reading aloud. "Okay, this is chapter 1, the first three verses that introduce the book as revealed by the apostle John when he was exiled on the isle of Patmos.

"'*The Revelation of Jesus Christ, which God gave Him to show His servants—things which must shortly take place. And He sent and signified it by His angel to His servant John, who bore witness to the word of God, and to the testimony of Jesus Christ, to all things that he saw. Blessed is he who reads and those who hear the words of this prophecy, and keep those things which are written in it; for the time is near.*'"

She looked up. "I never noticed before that it says those who read and hear the words of this prophecy and keep them are blessed, and the time is near." She paused before adding, "If the time was near two thousand years ago, it must be imminent now."

Phil digested this and then shook his head in agreement. "I'm glad you thought of Revelation right now. We sure need to hold onto our hope, with Ricky doing whatever he's into. Do you think Marie is a believer?"

Linda said thoughtfully, "I don't know. She and Bob go to church now and then, usually around the holidays. But she doesn't mention the Bible or God or anything like that. And she still uses profanity and makes crude jokes now and then. I mean, no one's perfect, right? But shouldn't there be some noticeable fruit to show whether she's saved or not?"

"Yes," Phil said emphatically. "Jesus said we will recognize other believers by their fruits or behaviors. Marie could be a baby Christian or not a believer at all. We have to keep praying for her."

"Let's do it now before we go any further in Revelation," Linda suggested.

The couple clasped hands as Phil began praying. "Dear Lord, please watch over Ricky and help him to recover fully. But also, please work in his life and his soul to make him aware of his need for salvation. And let someone come into his life who can get him to see the light. Also, please lead our daughter to realize her need for a Savior and make a faith commitment. We thank you for Nicholas's baptism last year and the evidence that shows he is a believer. Help us, dear Father, live as faithful servants to you, loving spouses to each other, and wise parents to our children. In Jesus's name, we pray. Amen."

"Thank you," Linda smiled, releasing her husband's hand. "Now let's get back into Revelation."

CHAPTER 3

"I don't know, Mom," Marie sighed into the phone. "Bob's been working an awful lot of overtime. I don't think we can get down to see you guys anytime soon."

"Are you sure?" Linda asked as she turned to look out the patio door at the colorful leaves falling from their backyard trees. "I know it would mean a lot to Ricky, to all of us, really. It's a bad time right now."

There was a pause before Marie answered, "I'll talk to him. But he thinks Ricky should have to pay for his mistakes instead of dragging everyone else into his problems. Is he going to rehab now?"

"Yes," Linda said, sitting down at the kitchen table. "Court ordered for two weeks. I just hope it helps this time." It was getting dark earlier these days, and she needed to start supper soon.

"Better keep that Jackal guy away from Ricky. he's the supplier for the gang."

"'Jackal'?" Linda wondered if she had heard right.

"Yeah, a clever nickname for 'Jack,' right? Thinks he's cool, but he's a jackal for sure, taking advantage of everybody in the neighborhood."

"How do you know this stuff?" Linda asked.

"Facebook, Instagram. His girlfriend friended me."

"Why? You don't hang around them, do you?" Linda said with concern in her voice.

"No, Mom." Marie sounded exasperated. "It's because I'm Ricky's sister, and she's checking up on him through me to tell Jackal in case Ricky tries to rat him out, but I don't tell her anything."

23

Linda felt drained. This was worse than she had imagined. "So Jackal is the pusher or supplier, whatever you called him, for Ricky and the rest of his gang. And if someone snitches to the cops—"

"Bang!" Marie roared. "But I don't think Ricky is going to turn him in unless the FDA guys push him for names."

Not yet fifty, Linda was feeling like a helpless old woman. Worrying over her son's drug addiction and gang involvement was terrible enough. Now to hear he could be killed if he were to inform on his drug supplier, she almost felt sick to her stomach.

"Mom?" Marie asked in concern. "You all right?"

"Yes," Linda said faintly, and then again in a louder voice, "it's just more than I expected. I shouldn't be surprised though. Your brother has always pushed the boundaries."

Thinking back for a second, a memory of her and Phil cuddling young Ricky after bringing him home from the hospital sent a wave of nostalgia through her. If only he had stayed that innocent.

"I kind of understand where Ricky is coming from," Marie said tentatively. "He wants to live on his own terms. He doesn't buy into all that church stuff that has grown on you and Dad over the years."

Glancing through the patio door again as the sun began to set over the distant hill, Linda said, "I get that. He needs to make his own decisions. But why does he make such terrible choices?" She shook her head in despair at her son's behavior.

"Didn't you ever make a mistake, Mom?" Marie said softly. "Something that you knew was wrong that hurt other people. Maybe your mom or grandparents?"

Thinking back to her youth, Linda did recall an incident that had shaken the foundation of her relationship with her mother. Linda had told her mom she was moving out at eighteen to live with a high school boyfriend who was also graduating. They had not been intimate yet, but that would come with the territory if they moved in together. Instead of panicking, her wise mother had sat Linda down and explained the real risks of such actions, which had scared Linda pretty good. Her mother then added the importance of making choices to please God rather than ourselves.

"He knows what's best," Sarah had explained to Linda. "He loves you and wants you to enjoy many good gifts on this earth but not at the expense of your faith or your integrity."

Although Linda wasn't wholly convinced, she agreed to wait until the end of that summer. During that time, she was accepted into the college of her choice and had gotten acquainted with some friends from church who were going to the same college. In a month, the live-in boyfriend episode disappeared and was replaced by excitement for college and a career.

"Yes," Linda said, returning to the present moment. "I almost made a bad decision that would have hurt my mother deeply and damaged my relationship with God. I'm so glad it didn't happen."

"But if it had," Marie continued, "your mother would still have loved you, right?"

"Of course," Linda said.

"And God would forgive you if you repented?"

"Yes," Linda replied, marveling at her daughter's wisdom.

"There you have it," Marie said triumphantly. "Love Ricky but not his actions. Never give up hope. Keep praying for him."

"I pray every day," Linda said. "How about you?"

"Sometimes, more often than not, I guess," Marie said. "I'm working on getting Bob to go to church with me. Maybe when the overtime dries up, he'll be ready."

They finished the call quickly, and Linda put a premade casserole in the oven. She mixed together a salad and made fresh lemonade. Phil and Nicholas arrived almost at the same time, and everyone sat down to dinner together. Only Ricky's seat was conspicuously empty.

"Let's pray," Phil said, and everyone bowed their heads.

"Dear Lord, thank you for keeping our family safe and for providing this comfortable home and delicious meal. We praise you for rescuing Ricky from another drug overdose. Please, heavenly Father, draw him close to you. Help him to remember and return to his childhood training. Bring believers into his life who will come alongside him and encourage him with the right words to turn him to you. In Jesus's name, amen."

After dinner, Nicholas went to basketball practice. Philip and Linda settled into their family room recliners and, for a moment, simply enjoyed the clear autumn night and the light breeze coming through the open window. As Linda shivered, Phil got up to close the window and sat down again.

"I love just relaxing like this," he said. "It's nice not having the TV on for a change."

Quiet settled over the room along with the dusky evening light, and Linda reached over to turn on the table lamp. As her eye caught the Bible left open to where they had left off previously, she said, "Do you feel like reading more of Revelation? There's plenty to think about in that book!"

"Sure," Phil said, reaching for the Bible. "We just barely got started in the first chapter, right?"

"Yes," Linda said. "I read the first few verses. That was quite an exciting introduction!"

"I remember. Let's see what comes next. My turn to read," Phil grinned. Taking the Bible onto his lap, he began reading slowly and firmly aloud.

"*'To him who loves us and has freed us from our sins by his blood, and has made us to be a kingdom and priests to serve his God and Father—to him be glory and power for ever and ever! Amen. Look, he is coming with the clouds, and every eye will see him, even those who pierced him; and all peoples on earth will mourn because of him. So shall it be! Amen. "I am the Alpha and the Omega," says the Lord God, "who is, and who was, and who is to come, the Almighty."'*"

He paused to let the words sink into both of their hearts.

Finally, Linda murmured, "Just think, believers will be 'a kingdom and priests.' Won't it be wonderful to serve a perfect King?"

"Amen," Phil said enthusiastically. "And to serve as priests before the Lord! I don't consider myself worthy for that role."

"But he has ordained it, honey. His blood cleansed our sins to make us fit for spiritual service. It's not something we could do for ourselves. God had to do it for us. All we can do is choose to accept his precious gift of salvation. It's amazing that so many people ignore or reject it."

Phil thought about it and then said, "We are blessed to be called his servants and children. I don't know how anyone could turn that down. Nothing here on earth comes close by comparison."

"I know," Linda said sadly. "If only our kids would understand God is reaching out to them to pull them back from the fire to save them from punishment for sins."

"I think it must be every Christian parent's greatest wish to see their children come to the Lord. It's mine for sure," Phil said. "I just wish Ricky would come to his senses. And I'm not sure about Marie. But at least they go to church sometimes."

"She does," Linda corrected. "Bob is working lots of overtime, but she's hoping he will go with her when his job slows down."

"Let's hope so. The world is becoming more of a terrible place every day. I hate to read the news headlines anymore. As was foretold, the world calls evil 'good' and good 'evil'. Things are getting turned upside down."

"And that keeps people from the Lord," Linda said. "If they're learning in school, at work, and around their communities that God is old-fashioned and the Ten Commandments have no place in public life, people think they can do anything they want and get away with it."

"That's exactly what they do," Phil sighed. "I've seen it at work where someone will lie on his resume or make up false references to get a promotion. Some of these so-called churches are more like dens of thieves, just like in Jesus's time, by taking people's money for personal use."

Suddenly, Phil's phone rang, startling the couple. Glancing at the phone, he said, "It's Reverend Skinner." Clicking to answer, he said, "Good evening, Pastor, how are you?"

The reverend replied, "I'm fine, Phil. How about you and Linda?"

"We're doing well, thanks for asking."

"Phil," Reverend Skinner began tentatively, "I was wondering if I could stop by and talk with you and Linda for a few minutes. It won't take long."

"Sure. Now? That's fine."

Linda nodded, assenting as Phil looked her way.

Ending the call, Phil asked, "I wonder what that's about at eight-thirty at night."

"Maybe he wants the deacons to do hospital visitations," Linda suggested.

"Could be," Phil said. "He'll be here in about ten minutes. That was a short Bible reading tonight. I like the next part in particular that says Jesus will come in the clouds and be seen by everyone on the earth, and all the nations will mourn because of him. Maybe that's because they're going to realize their guilt by not obeying God."

Linda got up to get some cookies for the reverend's visit. "Wow, that sounds incredible! I can't wait to see Jesus in the clouds, hopefully, one of these days soon."

"Me too," Phil said, laying the Bible aside and getting up to help his wife.

Just then, Nicholas came in through the side door, wearing his basketball jersey. "Hey, guys," he said, "we won!"

"I thought you would," Linda grinned and hugged her son.

"Good job! Must be those practice shots out in the driveway with your dad," Phil joked.

"Maybe," Nicholas smiled. "I'm going to take a shower." He dashed up the stairs.

A few minutes later, the doorbell rang. Phil answered and said, "Hi, Reverend Abel. Come on in and have a seat." He led the way to the family room and motioned for the pastor to sit down in an overstuffed chair near the two recliners.

Linda entered with a plate of cookies and some lemonade. "Here you go," she said, setting the treats on the coffee table within the reverend's reach.

"Thanks, Linda, that's very kind of you, but I'm trying to watch my weight." He patted his generous stomach.

She smiled politely as she and Phil sat down on the sofa, facing the reverend.

"I'm sure you're wondering what brings me here on a weeknight. Well, this is hard for me to say, but I'd best just be straightforward. The church board met Sunday night after Ricky was taken to the ER for his overdose. We all offer our support in this difficult situation. It's hard being a parent these days, and kids can be extremely challenging, especially when they get involved with the wrong crowd."

"So true," Phil said as Linda nodded.

"Before I say more, let's pray."

Everyone bowed their heads and closed their eyes as the reverend began to pray. "Heavenly Father, you know all things. You know that every believer does his or her best to follow your laws. As your church, we understand the importance of leading by example and showing others the path to salvation. We are mindful of your teachings in the Bible that inform us how to appoint church leaders. Please give us your wisdom in this meeting as we seek to serve your interests above all else. Amen."

Phil felt his stomach lurch.

Reverend Skinner spoke again. "Philip, you and Linda have served the church consistently with love and faith, maintaining a solid reputation and growing in your knowledge of the Lord. We were excited to have you become a deacon a few years ago, and you have not let us down."

He paused to find the right words. Linda gripped Phil's hand.

"The church board feels that, given the situation with Ricky, it is recommended that you step down from your deacon responsibilities until things work out with Ricky. We understand that he is a legal adult. But he has, until recently, lived under your roof." He stopped and looked at the couple with sympathy on his face. "When Ricky recovers from his addiction or makes a complete break from your home, that will be the time to resume your church responsibilities. First Timothy 3:12 teaches that a deacon should be faithful to his wife, which we believe to be true. Deacons must also manage their children and homes effectively. For the most part, you have done that, Phil. But Ricky's illicit and immoral behavior, while he remains part of your household, puts a barrier between you and church service. I trust it will be temporary, and you can deal with the problem soon. I know it's out of your hands to a great extent, but you may have to ask Ricky to move out."

"He doesn't stay here much anymore," Phil said thoughtfully. "Before his last episode, I don't think we saw him more than a couple of times a month."

"I understand," Reverend Skinner said. "Can you work out somewhere else for him to stay? If he's in rehab, they often have connections to halfway houses where residents are helped to find jobs and permanent housing."

"That would be really helpful," Philip said, brightening.

Linda breathed a sigh of relief.

All three stood up, and the men shook hands. Reverend Skinner said, "Thanks for letting me stop by on short notice. Gloria and I are praying for you and your family. Please let us know if you need anything."

"Thanks, we will," Phil said as he and Linda walked the pastor to the door just as Nicholas came bounding down the stairs. "Hi, Reverend Skinner!" he said.

"Hello, Nicholas! I stopped by the game tonight and noticed your team was ahead. Did you win?"

"We sure did!" Nicholas beamed.

"Well congratulations then, and keep the wins coming!"

As the door closed behind the reverend, Nicholas turned to face his parents. "I overheard the last part of the conversation between you and Reverend Skinner. I didn't mean to, but when I started down the steps, I heard him speaking in a serious voice, so I headed back up the steps but heard some of what he said. I'm sorry that Ricky's actions are impacting your deacon position, Dad. It shouldn't be this way."

"Pastor Kinner is right, son. The Bible is clear about the qualifications for church deacons and elders. I've been wondering what to do about Ricky, and the reverend gave us some ideas. Hopefully, we can help him get into a recovery program that will let him escape this addiction."

"Man, I hope so," Nicholas said, head lowered in disappointment for his father.

"It'll be okay," Philip smiled and put an arm around the boy's shoulders to hug him. "God always has a plan, as I continue to learn, so we will see where this leads. Maybe I needed an incentive to try harder to help Ricky. Let's pray about it right now."

Father, mother, and son stood in a circle in the foyer and clasped hands as Phil began to pray aloud, "Dear God, please strengthen our family for the challenges ahead. Work in Ricky's life to bring him close to you and be saved. Help us to know what we need to do to support his recovery. Equip me to be the husband and father I need to be for my family, and prepare me to resume my duties as a deacon in your timing. Amen."

As they parted to get ready for the next day, each realized, more than before, the urgency of Ricky getting help for his addiction and for each of them to prepare for the spiritual battles that were coming. It was more than Ricky; evil forces were at work to separate them from God and possibly from each other. They must be alert and stay grounded in the Word and pray faithfully for God's leading. The days and weeks ahead would not be easy, but Revelation had just reminded them that Jesus was going to return, and it would be glorious. They now must do their part to get ready and help others come to a saving knowledge of Jesus before it was too late.

CHAPTER 4

"What's the matter, Nicholas? You're not playing your usual game," Coach Demboldt said as he watched the young men moving around the court during practice.

The teenager paused and wiped the sweat from his face with his headband. "Nothing's wrong, just got a lot on my mind. That's all."

"Wanna talk about it?" the coach said in a low voice so the other players wouldn't hear.

Nicholas knew the coach was a good man and probably a Christian, but he didn't think it was a good idea to share family troubles with an outsider.

"Midterms are coming up in my college classes," Nicholas said. "I'm not that great at biology but hoping to pull at least a C."

The coach ambled over to where Nicholas was tossing foul shots. "No one's good at everything, son. Just do your best. There is a tutor on campus that might help by the name of Amy. Look her up on the website. I bet she can help you study for the test."

"Maybe. Thanks, coach." For the rest of the practice session, Nicholas gave his best effort. But he left feeling disappointed in himself and angry at his brother for disrupting the lives of everyone in the family. Even Marie was calling home every couple of days now instead of once or twice a month like before. Maybe it was good for her to stay in touch more often. Mom certainly appreciated it.

Driving home, Nicholas wondered how his dad really felt about stepping down from the deacon's role. Nicholas would have been straight-up embarrassed and upset. But his dad seemed to be taking it okay. He'd noticed that his father had become calmer and more patient over the past few years. Maybe it was due to his church involvement and the men's Bible study he went to regularly. Nicholas hoped he could be the man his father wanted him to become and not let him down like Ricky was doing.

In the following Sunday morning church service, Reverend Skinner stepped up to the pulpit after the praise and worship segment and gave the opening prayer. "Dear Father, bless us this day and forgive our shortcomings. Help us to be more like you. Give us wisdom and courage to stand up for what is right, and provide love and support for our church family. In Jesus's name, amen."

Everyone sat down as the reverend gazed out over the congregation. A ghost of a smile hovered around his lips as he recognized one face after another. These were his true spiritual family. Each one was special, and he had a pastoral duty to look after their well-being in whatever ways he could as their church leader.

"Today we are going to continue our study about Jesus's return," he began as Philip and Linda exchanged a quick smile. "But before we get started, I'd like to ask you to pray for Brother Philip and his wife, Linda, as well as their family. They are going through some issues right now and could use our prayer support."

A chorus of scattered "amen" responses sounded throughout the pews, with several shooting a sympathetic look at the couple sitting in the twelfth row near the back of the sanctuary, no longer in the customary fourth row for deacons. Nicholas sat beside his father but didn't look around.

Linda took her husband's hand, sensing his discomfort with being pointed out to everyone as needing prayer. She felt awkward as well, but she knew Reverend Skinner was doing what he felt best to support their family in this time of need. Leaning over to Phil, she whispered, "It's okay, honey. We need their prayers."

Reverend Skinner raised his hand solemnly and asked, "Will you pray with me?"

Everyone followed suit, and he stated firmly, "Lord God, we bring before you the Bullock family who need your loving-kindness and direction more than ever. Please watch over them, keep them safe, and bring them together in loving, healing, and unity."

"Amen" rang through the sanctuary as everyone looked up and opened their Bibles to the book of Revelation.

"This morning, we are going to look at Jesus's prophetic words found in Matthew 24 and 25. Please join me there."

The sound of numerous pages being turned could be heard with a few murmurs of someone whispering a comment or question about the topic.

"My brothers and sisters in Christ, our time here on earth grows short. The signs are everywhere as you have probably noticed for several years now. Like a woman in labor, the earth's pains are increasing in both intensity and frequency. I know some of you, ladies out there, can relate to this prophecy in particular."

"Oh yes" and "Preach it" could be heard here and there among the pews. Linda grinned and nodded as Phil caught her eye while Nicholas was reading the Matthew passages.

"Let us begin in Matthew 24 verses 3 through 8," Reverend Skinner said as he started to read aloud.

"'*Now as He sat on the Mount of Olives, the disciples came to Him privately, saying, "Tell us, when will these things be? And what will be the sign of Your coming, and of the end of the age?" And Jesus answered and said to them: "Take heed that no one deceives you. For many will come in My name, saying, I am the Christ, and will deceive many. And you will hear of wars and rumors of wars. See that you are not troubled; for all these things must come to pass, but the end is not yet. For nation will rise against nation, and kingdom against kingdom. And there will be famines, pestilences, and earthquakes in various places. All these are the beginning of sorrows.'*"

"Now let's break this down, verse by verse, to try and fully understand what Jesus was telling his disciples and those like us who would read his words when preserved in the Bible for generations to come. Verse 3 says that Jesus sat on the Mount of Olives where his disciples came to him privately. This was to be a training session, not a preaching session, to prepare his disciples for ministry. Similarly, let's look at these words and understand that Jesus spoke them for our benefit as well."

Several members of the congregation nodded and murmured in agreement. Phil put his arm around Linda's shoulders as they followed along in their Bibles while Reverend Skinner continued to read.

"Jesus's disciples...think of them now, James, John, Peter, Nathaniel, Matthew especially, who wrote this description of what happened, were all as eager as you and I to know what to expect. And they asked two questions that I'll rephrase in my own way for you. When are you coming back, Jesus? What will be the signs of your return and of the times that will be in place then?" Reverend Skinner paused and looked up at his congregation. "Are you asking those questions these days? I certainly am. I cannot wait to meet Jesus in the sky when he raptures his church out of this fallen world. But when will it happen? Let's continue." Looking at the Bible again, he repeated Jesus's words. 'Take heed that no one deceives you.' Did you hear that, church family? Someone, and we know who, is trying to deceive us. How do they do that? You've probably heard the lies 'Jesus was speaking metaphorically that his spirit would return, not him in the flesh' or 'Jesus was warning his disciples not to be deceived.' By whom? Me, your pastor? Your saved loved ones? The truly Christian evangelists and speakers you hear on television, radio, and online? No, that is what the evil one wants you to believe, to trust no one and so continue to be lost without hope of salvation." Looking around, the reverend noticed that everyone wore serious expressions.

They had heard the deceptions, and many had likely been mocked for their belief in Jesus's second coming.

Nicholas looked thoughtful. He had been teased and even bullied for his belief in Jesus and the coming rapture of believers.

"Jesus's next words warn us that many will come claiming to be Christ. Does he mean that literally? Most probably. There have been false prophets and teachers in the past, and there are some in the world now who say they are Jesus reincarnated as a different person or in a new body. Most people do not follow those figures who are just basically cult leaders."

He paused as several people nodded. Philip was thinking about a recent news headline announcing a new "messiah" somewhere in

Europe who was allegedly preparing the locals for aliens to come and transport them to another world. He shook his head in disgust.

Reverend Skinner continued. "But could Jesus also be referring to people who claim to be 'Christlike' and not just a literal savior?"

People nodded again with an occasional "yes" being heard around the room.

"I think so," Phil said to Linda, who nodded agreement.

"Absolutely," Nicholas whispered with the assurance of youth.

"We cannot say with certainty," Reverend Skinner explained. "But it does seem as if there are megachurch leaders who claim to have the key to salvation for a donation. Now I'm not saying all big churches are corrupt or led by deceptive pastors. I'm just saying, those that are that way are the most visible examples."

"Right," "true," and "yes" echoed here and there in response.

"But small churches or medium-size churches can likewise lead people astray when they don't adhere to the gospel of the Bible. Some folks want to change God's words or represent him as something he is not. They insist new believers must do this or that to be saved. But Jesus told Nicodemus that we just must be born again, confess our sins, and follow him as Lord and Savior. It's that simple. I'm not saying it's easy. Christians will each have to carry their own cross and bear one another's burdens. But God will be with us each step of the way."

"Amen" resounded across the sanctuary.

"'Many will be deceived,' Jesus told his disciples. Do we see that happening today? Yes, we do, with churches bending the Bible's rules or distorting them to fit their false image of a deity made to serve their interests. They have it all backward. The truth is that God came. First, he is all-powerful, and we are his subjects. He makes the rules, and we follow them."

"Amen" echoed even louder.

"Sadly, many people today are deceived, but they have allowed it. Instead of sticking to the Bible, they follow false leaders who give them a comfortable religion that promises much and requires little. Their pride will not let them admit they are wrong or change their views. So we must pray for them."

Thoughts of Ricky came to Nicholas as he recalled his older brother spewing distorted theology that he didn't even follow but threw it at Nicholas for argument's sake.

"People who claim to know God but follow a different doctrine than what is revealed as the inspired truth of God in the Bible are lost souls, having a form of faith but not true belief or trust. They will be the ones that Jesus will tell in the judgment, 'Depart from me. I never knew you.'"

Several murmured assent.

"Even within the Christian community, there are dissenters, deceivers, and unbelievers. Satan is actively recruiting more of those people for his dirty work of blocking the ones who truly are seeking God from finding salvation."

He paused and waited for that to sink in. Everyone listened intently except for eighty-six-year-old Vernon Jeffers sitting in the back row, who kept dozing off.

"Then Jesus described the sign of wars and rumors of wars. Do you know how many wars were fought in the twentieth century alone? It would be hard to count all the military conflicts throughout the world over the past one hundred years. But experts claim that the twentieth century was the bloodiest century for modern warfare and that World War II claimed the most lives. Somewhere between sixty-two and seventy-eight million people died."

A few gasps of surprise were heard, along with a couple of groans.

The reverend continued. "So I believe it is safe to assume that the wars and rumors of war that continue to grow in the first couple decades of the twenty-first century are the fulfillment of Jesus's prophecy. There are more wars than ever, and we read about wars—occurring or imminent—in the news each day. There's no escaping it."

Many people nodded.

"But there is good news too. The end is not yet here. Jesus said not to be troubled because these things must come—country against country, kingdom versus kingdom. We see it now, and more is coming. That tells us that God is in control."

Near audible sighs could be heard, some of relief and others of vexation about the continued warfare.

"Moreover," Reverend Skinner went on, "there will be famines. I know some of you send donations to places with high poverty rates to help feed the hungry. Jesus said the poor would always be with us, and that has proven true. Pestilences mean diseases. We have new diseases being discovered by science all the time. Ebola, Zika virus, Lyme disease, COVID-19. More will likely develop and attack humans. Earthquakes have been around since the earth's formation, and geologists have only begun accurately measuring them in recent times. Many earthquakes are occurring around the world at any given time. In Yellowstone National Park, geysers and rumblings remind us of the vast caldera lying beneath the earth's surface that could erupt at almost any time. Other earthquakes are exploding in various countries and causing serious damage to life and property."

More nods confirmed the congregation's agreement with the reverend's words.

"Are we there yet? Is the rapture about to happen? Well, it could. No one knows the date or time. But Jesus reminds us that these are but 'the beginning' of sorrows on the earth. More will come. We must be watchful, as Jesus told his disciples in another passage with the parable of the ten virgins with the lamps. Only one of the ten brought enough oil to light her lamp while waiting for the bridegroom. The other nine were shut out of the festivities because they were not prepared. Were the people of Noah's time ready for the flood? No. They didn't believe righteous Noah, and they drowned in the deluge. What about the people of Sodom and Gomorrah? No, again, as they laughed at Lot and his family and tried to assault them. But God sent two angels to rescue Lot and his daughters while his wife looked back and was turned to a pillar of salt."

Everyone appeared to be digesting this information thoughtfully.

"Brothers and sisters, are you ready for the ark? Will you escape the brimstone? Are you going to be raptured with the church or left behind in the tribulation? I beseech you to prayerfully consider your eternal destiny by reading these words of Jesus again at home, meditating on them, and praying over them. Next week, we will conclude our study of Matthew 24, considering Jesus's teachings on the end-times, and we will begin Matthew 25. Until then, be vigilant for your souls. Let no one deceive you. Stand fast in your love for the Lord."

As he closed the sermon in prayer, everyone listened and prayed with their pastor. They could now see how close Jesus's return was as well as the destruction that was coming that they must avoid. They had to do everything possible to help the unsaved turn to God for salvation.

During the car ride home, Nicholas asked questions about the sermon and how the end-times would play out.

"I think we're there," Phil said thoughtfully as he steered the car down their street. "Not that the rapture is going to happen today, but it could. I mean that the world is changing dramatically, and we have to be prepared to withstand the pressures that will come and the troubles afflicting us already."

"Right," Linda said. "Ricky is perplexed at this time. We have to do what we can to show him love and be ready with answers if he asks questions about God or the Bible."

"I don't know if he wants to hear the answers we can give him," Phil said evenly.

"We have to try if he lets us," Linda replied gently.

"I'll try to get together with him soon," Nicholas promised.

"I called about the halfway house," Linda said. "They have an opening if Ricky wants it. His caseworker in the recovery program is going to discuss it with him."

"Let's hope this works out," Nicholas said. "I want to see my brother in heaven someday."

"We can always pray. And we should make Ricky's salvation a priority, which I know we've been doing," Phil said as the car turned into the driveway. He put it in park and turned off the ignition. "Reverend Skinner made it clear that the world is going to see some nasty changes, and Ricky may not be ready to deal with them. Social turbulence or bad personal choices could send him spiraling out of control again. I just wish we could get him away from that gang he runs with."

"Jackal is still recruiting new members, so maybe the gang isn't holding together too well," Nicholas offered. Linda didn't want to ask how he knew, but she assumed he got his information from social media connections.

"I've seen the end-times in progress for a while now," Phil said thoughtfully as they got out of the car. "People want to do things their way. Greedy, selfish, disrespectful. Not everyone, of course, but too many for comfort. We have to be examples of Christ-like love and behavior," he reminded them.

As Linda unlocked the front door and they entered, she said, "I see it too. The signs are all around us, and they're getting more noticeable. I'm excited and a little scared."

"Me too," Nicholas said as he prepared to go upstairs and change out of his church clothes.

"I think we all are," Phil said. "We'll need plenty of prayer cover daily."

CHAPTER 5

"Hi, are you—"

"Amy," the slender girl with deep brown eyes said as she stood up and offered her hand. "You must be Nicholas. At least that's who's scheduled for my four o'clock appointment. Sit down." She gestured to the chair next to hers around a large roundtable that could seat four.

"Yes, Nicholas Bullock. Nice to meet you." As he sat down and opened his backpack, Amy asked, "Would you like a soda or a cup of coffee?" She gestured to the half-full coffeepot sitting on a sideboard with cups, stir sticks, and creamer.

"Oh, no thanks," Nicholas smiled. This was a more casual environment than he had expected, never having met with a tutor before.

Amy resumed her seat and waited expectantly as Nicholas pulled out his biology textbook and a notebook that he opened to a biology tab. Thumbing through, he found his assignment and placed it on the table near Amy.

She glanced over the guidelines and then at the lab report that Nicholas pulled out of the folder. Skimming it, she said, "Don't you need to add the methodology for the experiment?" Her face was serious, but her eyes were kind and thoughtful.

Nicholas liked how her hair was braided, so neat and feminine somehow. Forcing himself to focus on the assignment, he glanced over his lab report again and saw what Amy meant.

"That's right. I do need to add the methodology. How could I have missed that?"

"We all do things like that sometimes," she said reassuringly. "Do you know how to set one up?"

"Yeah, I've done a couple in this class already. I can work on it tonight."

"Problem solved!" Amy grinned.

Nicholas was just starting to feel comfortable and in no hurry to leave. "How long have you been a tutor here?"

"This is my second year," Amy replied. "So far, I've been blessed to get mostly hardworking students who are eager to learn."

The word "blessed" caught Nicholas's attention. Could she be a Christian? Glancing at the clock, he noticed they had about ten minutes left before his tutoring session was up. Amy didn't seem in any hurry to end the session either. As they made casual conversation, Nicholas found out that she was a nursing student, which was why she was good at biology. She and her parents and another sister in middle school lived in a neighborhood not too far from where Nicholas's family lived.

When the receptionist stopped by their table to mention that the next appointment had arrived, Nicholas got up reluctantly and picked up his backpack.

"Come back any—" Amy started to say as Nicholas blurted, "Can I come back if I need more help?" They chuckled at the overlap.

"Thanks," Nicholas said warmly. "I'll probably see you before long. Biology isn't my thing."

"No problem," Amy smiled. "I'll be here."

A skinny boy with saggy jeans and a hoodie covering his face made his way toward the elementary school playground that was deserted as twilight descended over the city. Hands shoved in his pockets, he had left the stolen car at home and taken the bus to avoid being pulled over and caught. He would drive the vehicle openly after it was painted by one of the gang members whose stepdad used to work in an autobody shop and had surplus supplies sitting in the garage. Another bro was making a counterfeit title for the car by piecing together a fake document from the computer. Now all he needed was a little more cash to cover these expenses, and everything would be fine.

Crossing the blacktop parking lot of the school, the teenager looked around to ensure no police or security vehicles were parked nearby. The adjacent street was empty as the streetlights overhead began to glow. Moving toward the swings, the lanky youth sat down in one of them and pulled a tissue from his pocket. Carefully opening it, he held it up to his nostrils and inhaled deeply. The substance rushed to his brain, immediately quelling his anxiety while stoking a sense of euphoria. *Ahh...great stuff.* Pushing the tissue back into his hoodie pouch, he saw from the corner of his eye someone approaching from the other side of the playground near the slide. He recognized the height and build of his protégé, Ricky, who was determined would join the gang and earn his rank by serving the leader.

"Whassup?" the stockier teen whispered as he got within earshot.

"Not much, bro. Did ya bring it?"

"Yeah, Jackal, it's right here." The new arrival fished in his pocket and pulled out a 9mm semiautomatic handgun, cautiously showing the prize to his mentor and manipulator.

The thin boy reached out and took it. "Okay, man, not bad." Tucking it into his pouch with the tissue, he asked, "You want some stuff?"

Ricky shook his head. "Can't, man, I'm broke. Ain't worked for a week now, and my old man won't give me nothin'."

"Shoot him, and you'll get his money," Jackal snorted.

Ricky hid his shock. "It ain't like that, bro. My old man's a good guy, just not with it, you know?"

"Oh yeah," Jackal sniffed, feeling the last of the drug pulsing through his body. "Sometimes, the shoe goes on the other foot. We gotta teach the parents to respect their offspring." He giggled, and Ricky tried not to recoil.

"I'll get some money and meet you here in a couple of days."

Jackal's eyes narrowed as he stepped closer to Ricky and caught the smell of alcohol. "I got stuff for you. Don't make me waste it. My supplier don't take no returns."

"Yeah, I got you." Ricky turned to leave as Jackal roughly grabbed his arm.

"You hear me, boy? I ain't messin' wit' you. Get back here by Thursday, or I and the bros will find you."

"Okay." Ricky shrugged off the hand and left, head bowed, wondering how he ever got mixed up with this hoodlum. As he strode off down the street under the streetlights, he felt like a sewer rat running the dark streets for survival. He was too ashamed to go to his parents for help.

*****

Philip got up early the following day and turned the automatic coffee maker to the low setting that would keep the coffee hot for Linda. Pouring himself a cup and adding a splash of creamer, he went into the dining room and glanced outside at the misty morning sunrise. The neighborhood was quiet, the way Phil liked it. He pulled open his Bible and began reading in Matthew 24 where Reverend Skinner had left off in Sunday's sermon.

> *And Jesus answered and said to them: "Take heed that no one deceives you. For many will come in My name, saying, 'I am the Christ,' and will deceive many. And you will hear of wars and rumors of wars. See that you are not troubled; for all these things must come to pass, but the end is not yet. For nation will rise against nation, and kingdom against kingdom. And there will be famines, pestilences, and earthquakes in various places. All these are the beginning of sorrows.*
>
> *Then they will deliver you up to tribulation and kill you, and you will be hated by all nations for My name's sake. And then many will be offended, will betray one another, and will hate one another. Then many false prophets will rise up and deceive many. And because lawlessness will abound, the love of many will grow cold. But he who endures to the end shall be saved. And this gospel of the kingdom*

will be preached in all the world as a witness to all the nations, and then the end will come."

"Wow," Philip unconsciously said aloud as he looked up after reading the passage.

"What?" Linda asked from the doorway after hearing her husband's voice. She was dressed for work and walked into the kitchen to pour herself some coffee.

"Unbelievable," Phil said. "Although I've read this chapter many times before, since hearing the reverend's sermon, it's suddenly taking on more meaning."

Linda came into the dining room with her coffee and took a seat across from Phil. "Really? Like which parts?" She sipped from the steaming mug.

"All of it," Phil said. "So much is happening in the world right now to show Jesus's prophecies are coming true. Everyone is too busy to notice. That must be Satan's doing."

"You mean like the wars and famines, things like that?" Linda asked with interest.

"Right," Phil said after sipping his coffee. "But those things seem so remote from most of us here in the US. We have a pretty cushy life. Disasters on that scale don't necessarily affect us here much. Maybe the price of gas or food items goes up sometimes, but that's about it."

"So what does affect us here and now?" Linda asked with interest.

Phil read aloud to his wife the verses he had just read silently to himself as she listened attentively. When he finished, she said thoughtfully, "So we will be hated and persecuted."

"It's coming," Phil said. "Don't you sense it? Do you feel like you have to keep quiet about your faith to avoid people scoffing at or ridiculing you?"

She nodded. "I'm ashamed to admit it, but yes, I do. I need to open up and share the gospel with those who want to hear the good news."

"It's risky," Phil said. "No one in the accounting office wants to talk about the Bible or church. They're just into sports scores and off-color jokes. If I bring up faith-based topics, well, they politely excuse themselves and leave."

"That happens to me too!" Linda said.

"In the footnote to the passage, there's a cross-reference to other prophecies. Listen to this from 2 Timothy 3 verses 1 through 7." He read aloud, "*But know this, that in the last days perilous times will come: For men will be lovers of themselves, lovers of money, boasters, proud, blasphemers, disobedient to parents, unthankful, unholy, unloving, unforgiving, slanderers, without self-control, brutal, despisers of good, traitors, headstrong, haughty, lovers of pleasure rather than lovers of God, having a form of godliness but denying its power. And from such people turn away! For of this sort are those who creep into households and make captives of gullible women loaded down with sins, led away by various lusts, always learning and never able to come to the knowledge of the truth.*"

"Perilous times," Linda repeated when Phil finished. "I think those times are here. Crime rates are accelerating, families are turning against each other, and it seems like the human race is going backward rather than forward in the way they treat each other."

Phil agreed. "Think about the new stories we hear of people doing terrible things for money to serve their own interests. They break in and steal and even kill family members for money or lust. Others do it from greed or because they are desperate to support their drug habit. And if you've noticed the music lyrics kids are listening to today, some are unbelievable. The performers boast about seeking fame and money, and sex is treated as a game rather than a commitment."

"It's no wonder single-parent families are growing in number," Linda said sadly. "The poor kids are lost and take to the streets to find self-worth and family-type support."

"In all the wrong places," Phil agreed. "Disobedient to parents and headstrong. Ricky fits that to a T."

"He used to be a good son," Linda said after another sip of coffee. "I don't know what happened."

"I think he got in with the wrong crowd," Phil said. "I know those lost kids in the gang need help too, but right now, I'm concerned about our son."

"I guess all of us have some of those traits," Linda mused. "We need to be aware of our shortcomings and repent of them to God. He'll forgive anyone who asks."

"Lovers of pleasure rather than lovers of God," Phil added. "Think of all the people who don't care about God. They put him out of the schools, out of the government, out of sight everywhere. They're just interested in this world, not the next, and cater to their bodies, not their souls."

"We have to be careful not to fall into that pit too," Linda cautioned. "I mean, I don't think we're putting the world ahead of God, but it's a huge trap that catches plenty of people. I know I've been guilty of overspending and charging too much on our credit cards." She paused. "You know what? Let's put all the cards away and just use one. We can pay down those balances and be better stewards of the things God has given us."

"Honey, that's a great idea," Philip said enthusiastically. "I'd love to keep our monthly budget under control and build up our savings for emergencies. Do you want to revise our monthly expenses to see what we can do?"

"Sure," Linda said, happy that Phil trusted her with this critical task since she had been prone to overspending in the past. It was a sign of the healthy growth of their marriage in a godly direction. When they learned to manage their income wisely, God might give them more responsibilities of a spiritual nature to manage. She added, "We don't want to be the kind of Christians that have a 'form' of godliness but deny its power. We're blessed to have a Bible-based pastor like Reverend Skinner."

"He is great," Philip agreed. Inwardly, he was still slightly hurt about being asked to resign from the deacon position, but he knew it was for the best. He and Linda would continue trying to figure out how to help their son Ricky get his life together. Then he could see about being reinstated as a deacon when the time was right.

Linda got up. "It's time to go. I'll grab a fruit bar for breakfast to eat at work. Have some juice or toast before you leave," she suggested.

"I better eat something. The docs say it's better for your health not to skip breakfast."

He got up and came over to his wife, giving her a big hug. "Have a blessed day, sweetie."

"You too."

"Hey, Marie," Bob called as he was heading out the door to his car. "You wanna have dinner with the Crawfords tonight? They texted me again."

"Oh yeah, that could work," Marie said as she came downstairs, brushing her hair. "I guess so. I mean, we should be friendly with our neighbors, right?"

Bob paused in the doorway. "Yeah, but we don't really know them. What's the point?"

Marie walked over to her husband and kissed his cheek. "That's the point, silly. We can get to know them over dinner. It'll be nice to get acquainted with people in the neighborhood."

"Okay, I'll let them know we can make it at 6:00 p.m. at Leeland's. I'll meet you there since it's close to my job."

"Great, see you there!"

Over delectable steak dinners that evening, the two couples chatted about their jobs, the suburban neighborhood, the gorgeous fall weather, and sports. All but Desiree Crawford opted for dessert, choosing neither chocolate mousse nor apple strudel.

"I can't," she said, chuckling. "Or I won't be able to get up from this table."

Marie marveled at the woman's slender figure and self-control. Leeland's was known for its signature desserts, and she, for one, was not going to pass them up.

"So," Mel Crawford said as he forked bites of the tender strudel, "do you two attend church somewhere?"

Bob and Marie exchanged glances. "We go with my parents sometimes," Marie offered. But our work shifts don't always let us attend. What about you two? Are you members anywhere?"

"Yes," Desiree smiled, "we've been going to Truth Temple for about six years now. It's a lovely small church with selected membership, maybe thirty or forty families. We'd love to have you go with us one of these days."

"Well," Marie said carefully, "we could possibly do that. What denomination is the church?"

"Nondenominational," Mel offered. "No rigid requirements or strange rituals. Just simple faith."

"Sounds good," Bob said. "We'll give it a try."

"How about this Sunday?" Desiree gently pressed, with her gracious smile.

"What time?" Marie asked.

"Eleven a.m., so you can sleep in a little before the service," Desiree added.

Marie glanced at Bob and said, "Okay, we'll meet you there."

"Oh, we can drive since we know the way, and you can save your gas," Mel offered.

"Thanks, we'll be at your place at ten-thirty," Marie said. "Informal attire, or is there a dress code?"

"Informal is fine," Desiree said. "It'll be nice having you with us."

For some reason, Marie felt a cold chill go down her back, but she could not imagine why. The Crawfords seemed like a lovely young couple and had not yet started their family, like Marie and Bob. So it was natural they would have the time to be involved in their church. They almost seemed...too nice. Marie reprimanded herself silently for the suspicious thought and smiled at the Crawfords.

On the drive home, she asked Bob, "Are you okay with church this Sunday?"

Bob yawned. "Oh, you know how I am. Church isn't that important to me. But if it will make you happy and help us connect to them, I guess I can tolerate an hour of a Sunday lecture."

"It's a sermon, not a lecture," Marie said as she playfully jabbed her husband's arm with her elbow. "We can try it once, and if we don't like it, we'll make an excuse not to go again."

"Sounds good," Bob said.

CHAPTER 6

"Hang on a minute," the middle-aged, slightly overweight man panted. "Let me catch up."

The leaner man who was jogging the trail ahead of his friend slowed his pace and then stopped, bending over to catch his breath as the other caught up. "I guess I was going a little faster than usual, Reverend Abel. Sorry about that."

"No problem, Phil," the reverend said, no longer panting but breathing a bit hard. "I need to be challenged more like that. Got to get this belly down." He patted his rounded paunch and grinned.

"Well it's good for both of us," Phil said, looking around. "And I appreciate you're meeting with me on these weekly runs." He looked around at the beautiful park setting where other runners and bicyclists were getting a morning workout and then checked his smart watch. "That's about two miles so far. Should we stop?"

"I don't mind if you don't," the pastor said, wiping his face with the towel that was looped over the tie cord of his sweatpants. "Do you have time to sit down for a few minutes at that picnic table?" He pointed to one under the shade of a large, silver maple tree with leaves that were starting to turn vibrant shades of yellow, orange, and red.

"Sure, I just have to be back at the house for a quick shower before work," Phil said.

The pair made themselves comfortable on the wooden seats. Pastor Skinner looked at his long-time friend with compassion and affection. "How's everything going?"

"Fine," Phil said, meaning it. "My job is keeping me busy as we rev up for a new season of research after the first of the year. Linda has been offered a training position at the hospital, which will mean a promotion if she takes it. She's giving serious thought to the responsibilities that come with the job, but I think she would make a great instructor for nursing students."

"That's good news," Pastor Abel said, smiling. "Nicholas evidently met with Amy Brown, a young lady who tutors college students in science classes. Or maybe I shouldn't be letting the cat out of the bag?" he added.

"Oh, no problem," Phil said. "Nicholas mentioned it over dinner the other night. We're glad he's smart enough to get help when needed." He paused, looking for the right words. "I just wish Ricky would do the same."

"No progress yet? Gloria and I have been praying for him and for your family."

"Thanks, reverend. That means a lot. Sometimes it feels like a lonely, uphill battle. But we know Jesus is right there with us."

"So true. Things will work out the way...the way God ordains them," the pastor said in a reassuring tone.

"Linda and I are reading through the book of Revelation. We've just started chapter 2, but man, it's exciting. Kind of makes me fearful and hopeful at the same time, if that makes sense."

"I think most of us feel the same way," Reverend Abel said, nodding. "This Sunday, I plan to continue our study of Jesus's end-time prophecies from Matthew 25. He said some awesome things about what's coming. And I have to tell you, I need to warn our church family to be ready for a wave of seismic events. Of course, neither I nor anyone else knows exactly when things will take place, but one of the key aspects is convergence, in other words, when several things begin to happen around the same time and fall into a pattern that leads right into the final events of earthly existence as we know it."

"Really?" Phil was amazed. "I want to hear you preach on that! I've read Matthew several times, and I'm aware of the prophecies Jesus spoke of. But I'm eager to hear your take on his words."

"The first part is about the ten virgins who were waiting for the bridegroom to arrive so they could join the wedding party. But some weren't ready. Five forgot to bring oil for their lamps, so they had to go right before midnight to buy oil, while the other five were ready with lamps lit by the oil they had brought. While the others left to buy oil, the bridegroom came, and everyone went into the feast except the virgins who were not ready. Half their number, 50 percent, were unprepared. I surely hope that is not the percentage of unprepared people in our church. But if so, we must help to prepare them."

Philip grinned. "I can't wait to hear more."

"Be there this Sunday, and you'll hear every word," the reverend smiled. Getting serious again, he added, "I'm sorry about your stepping down from church deaconship, Phil. You're a good man, and you have served our congregation faithfully for years. I believe the Lord will restore your position in an abundance of recognition and celebration in his timing."

Although it was a touchy subject, Phil appreciated the reverend's kind words of faith.

"Thanks, Reverend Abel. I hope so."

Linda Bullock was entering patient notes from the morning hospital rounds when the director of nursing appeared at the nursing station. "Good morning, Linda. I see you're as busy as always. That's a good look," she teased.

"I might not always feel it," Linda said, glancing up, "but I give it my best."

"I know you do, and that's what I'm here about. Do you have some time to talk about the clinical instructor position?"

"Of course," Linda said. "I can make time now if that works with your schedule. I don't think anyone's using the conference room."

"Great, that works for me."

The two women headed down the hall. In the conference room, the DON closed the door. "This won't take long, Linda. I just want to go over a few things with you about the new position."

"I appreciate you're doing that before I actually start next week, Mrs. Stephens. I'm grateful for your confidence in my ability to do a good job, and we all want the transition to be seamless."

As they settled into the comfortable padded seats, Mrs. Stephens began. "You've always performed stellar work with patients and staff, Linda. That's why we feel lucky to move you to the instructor's position."

"Thank you, Mrs. Stephens. I enjoy working with people and try to make them as comfortable as possible in what can be challenging medical circumstances."

"Exactly. As nursing professionals, we all have different ways of encouraging and supporting patients who may be experiencing a life-changing event or significant discomfort." She paused as though measuring her words. "But as you know, Linda, matters of faith are personal. Although we respect your right to the religious beliefs of your choice, we cannot allow staff to share their beliefs here at the hospital. The chaplain handles that. It was brought to my attention that you prayed with the teenage daughter of a woman who was dying from car accident injuries."

"Yes," Linda agreed, her cheeks warming. "The girl was distraut, and I wanted to help her cope with her mother's passing. No family members were there, and she was taking it hard."

"I understand," Mrs. Stephens said. "But we cannot breach protocol for any circumstances. You could have hugged her without mentioning Jesus or God. You might have directed her to the chaplain's office or found a staff member to stay with her until a relative arrived."

"She was heartbroken," Linda said, inwardly stunned by the lack of compassion for the young girl. "She asked me to pray with her. I couldn't say no."

Mrs. Stephens listened, her face impassive, and then replied, "It was a difficult situation, and your reaction—spontaneous. Let's hope there are no more of those. If you want to remain employed with us, Linda, you will need to keep your religious views silent."

Linda silently absorbed this information, outwardly calm but inwardly agitated. While she understood and complied with the hospital policy against proselytizing, this had been an exceptional case. The girl was distressed as the brain and heart monitors on her mother's unconscious form slowed and then stopped. What else could she have done? Suddenly, Linda felt emotionally exhausted. How could she remain faithful to her beliefs if she must stay quiet when people needed to hear them most?

"Thank you for clarifying the hospital's position, Mrs. Stephens," Linda said politely. "I will keep that in mind."

Mrs. Stephens got up and smiled. "I knew we could count on you. I think you'll make a wonderful instructor."

Linda took her supervisor's hand, shook it lightly, and then followed her out of the conference room where the two parted ways in the hall. Returning to her workstation and dictation equipment at the nurses' station, she recalled a Bible passage from the women's study she had attended a few weeks ago. While she did not have it memorized, she had studied the verses often enough to have a firm grasp on the meaning of Matthew 25, which coincidentally was where Reverend Skinner would be preaching the following Sunday.

As she understood it, Jesus had compared the kingdom of heaven to a man traveling a great distance. Before he left, he gave five talents to a servant, two to another, and the third servant received just one. The three servants were to make good use of those talents, a unit of money, to earn more. The first two servants invested their talents and doubled the value. But the servant who received one hid it in the ground so that its value remained the same.

Settling herself in the chair where she would resume posting notes about the patients she had seen that morning, Linda recalled the outcome of Jesus's parable. The master of the estate returned after a long time and asked each servant to give an account. The two servants who had doubled the value of their talents were given more responsibilities to oversee that demonstrated the master's trust and faith in them. "Enter into the joy of your lord."

If only Mrs. Stephens had said *that* to her today instead of warning her to hide her faith!

Then Linda recalled the words of the third servant who seemed to whine in explaining he had hidden his one talent: "I was afraid and went and hid your talent in the ground." Isn't that what Mrs. Stephens was asking Linda to do—hide her talent, her beloved faith, from those who needed it most?

Now Linda recalled the response of the master in the parable who represented God: "You wicked and lazy servant. You knew that I reap where I have not sown and gather where I have not scattered seed. Take the talent from him and." She struggled to remember the lazy servant's fate. Then it came to her: "And cast the unprofitable servant into the outer darkness. There will be weeping and gnashing of teeth." She shuddered at the memory of his destiny. Would she face the same judgment if she hid her faith from the world?

Pushing aside her anxious thoughts, Linda prayed in her mind, *Dear Lord, help me to do your will.*

That night over dinner, she told Phil about the meeting with the director of nursing. "She was nice," Linda said. "But she definitely wants to put a stop to any prayers, Bible reading, or talk of faith."

Phil sat back and shook his head. "It's going to get worse. The world is pushing God further and further away, along with those of us who serve God and represent his interests on earth. They don't understand or care we are trying to save them from eternal suffering. The gospel message is nonsense to them."

Linda finished chewing the bite of casserole and swallowed it before answering. "It's sad. People are dying without hearing God's message of love and salvation."

Phil said, "I'm sure God provides some way for them to hear about the gospel, but he always leaves it up to the person to choose him or not. We can only do our best as opportunities present and leave the rest to the Holy Spirit and the individual."

"Like Ricky," Linda said softly.

"Yes," Phil agreed.

Four youths dressed in white T-shirts, dark baggy pants, and black hoodies gathered at the far end of a deserted parking lot under a leafy oak tree that was shedding colorful leaves in the evening breeze. Jackal quickly handed out capsules and rolled cigarettes with his right hand that continually dipped into his hoodie pouch and collected their money with his left hand. In moments, the pack of teenagers was swallowing, sniffing, and smoking a variety of substances while Jackal counted the bills he had received and stuffed them in a money belt at his waist under the hoodie.

"Hey, where's Ricky," one boy asked, looking around.

"He's comin'," Jackal said with assurance, although he was privately wondering if Ricky would show. Jackal could smell uncertainty a mile away, and Ricky had that distinctive air about him. *He could be swayed either way...*

Jackal's phone beeped a text message that he speedily read, "Waiting on $." The gang leader wondered if that meant Ricky would show or was putting him off indefinitely.

"Ricky's old man is a biological researcher, right?" he asked no one in particular.

"I heard sompin' like dat," a tall teen said, swaying a little.

In his mind, Jackal was playing different scenarios. Ricky could get access to his dad's assets one way or another if he wanted to. Jackal would find a way to spur Ricky's efforts to claim those assets. He needed cash, and Ricky would make a handy conduit.

*****

By Sunday morning, the congregation was restless and ready for Pastor Skinner's sermon on Matthew 25. They had read the news stories: Natural disasters had increased 25 percent over the past twenty years; fewer Americans believed the Bible was literal truth; more youth were turning away from church and belief in God. People of all ages seated in the pews *needed* their pastor's leadership to stoke their faith and keep them committed to their daily walk with the Lord.

"Good morning, church family," Pastor Abel Skinner began as he looked around the auditorium and smiled at the members. "Good to be back together again, worshipping our God and his risen Son, Jesus Christ!"

Shouts of "amen" and "yes" filled the air. As the reverend led them through the morning prayer, followed by the choir performing several uplifting hymns, the congregation's hearts were lifted and revived.

"Are you glad to be here?" Reverend Skinner asked as the music slowed to the stop, and he took the pulpit again.

"Yes" and "Yes, sir" could be heard around the large room.

"Today, as promised, we are going to look at Matthew 25 and Jesus's teachings about the end-times. None of us should be caught unaware. We must be ready for Jesus's return, which could be any moment. Moreover, we must prepare for the judgment that is coming—one for the saved and another for the unsaved. 'For by faith are you saved by grace. It is the gift of God, not of works, lest any man should boast,' he recited as several members in the audience murmured agreement.

"Amen," Phil said, taking Linda's hand. Nicholas smiled to see his parents' gesture of affection.

"Now let's begin by reading Matthew 25, verses 31 through 46. Please read silently along with me.

"*'When the Son of Man comes in His glory, and all the holy angels with Him, then He will sit on the throne of His glory. All the nations will be gathered before Him, and He will separate them one from another, as a shepherd divides his sheep from the goats. And He will set the sheep on His right hand, but the goats on the left. Then the King will say to those on His right hand, "Come, you blessed of My Father, inherit the kingdom prepared for you from the foundation of the world: for I was hungry and you gave Me food; I was thirsty and you gave Me drink; I was a stranger and you took Me in; I was naked and you clothed Me; I was sick and you visited Me; I was in prison and you came to Me." Then the righteous will answer Him, saying, "Lord, when did we see You hungry and feed You, or thirsty and give You drink? When did we see You a stranger and take You in, or naked and clothe You? Or when did we see You sick, or in prison, and come to You?" And the King will answer and say to them, "Assuredly, I say to you, inasmuch as you did it to one of the least of these My brethren, you did it to Me." Then He will also say to those on the left hand, "Depart from Me, you cursed, into the everlasting fire prepared for the devil and his angels: for I was hungry and you gave Me no food; I was thirsty and you gave Me no drink; I was a stranger and you did not take Me in, naked and you did not clothe Me, sick and in prison and you did not visit Me." Then they also will answer Him, saying, "Lord, when did we see You hungry or thirsty or a stranger or naked or sick or in prison, and did not minister to You?" Then He will answer them, saying, "Assuredly, I say to you, inasmuch as you did not do it to one of the least of these, you did not do it to Me." And these will go away into everlasting punishment, but the righteous into eternal life."'*

The congregation was so intently following along with the pastor's reading aloud that no one noticed the skinny boy in the dark hoodie who slipped in through the back of the sanctuary and took a seat in a pew by himself.

CHAPTER 7

"Mornin', Mr. and Mrs. Bullock," the skinny teen with the baggy clothes said politely as the congregation was dispersing toward the back of the sanctuary and out the main doors. Old Man Jeffers was stirred awake by the voice across the aisle. Getting up, he used his cane to move toward the exit.

Philip and Linda exchanged a surprised look, while Nicholas's face wore a question mark.

"Good morning. Have we met before?" Philip asked evenly, ushering the teen and his family toward a side aisle to keep from blocking other members from exiting the church.

"No, sir, I don't believe so. My name is Jack Handel, and I'm friends with your son Ricky." He offered his hand, which Philip accepted and shook. He had never expected to see the disreputable gang member at church; maybe God was working in the boy's heart?

"Hey, Jackal," Nicholas murmured, offering his hand, which the other boy took somewhat less agreeably.

"Yeah, Jackal's my street—I mean, the name my friends use," he offered, correcting himself. "Because you know, I'm fast on my feet."

"Right," Nicholas said knowingly without argument to avoid controversy.

"I was wondering if I could talk to you folks about Ricky. I am, um, kind of concerned about him."

Surprised again, Philip glanced at Linda who nodded almost imperceptibly. She said, "We have dinner at home waiting in the crockpot. Can you join us?"

"Sure," Jackal grinned. "Will Ricky be there?"

"No, I'm afraid not," Philip said.

"That's okay. We can talk openly," the teen said, using his best grammar. He could be polished when needed, which on occasion served his interests well.

"Sure," Philip said. He scribbled the family's home address on the church bulletin and handed it to the young man. "We'll be there in about fifteen minutes."

"See you then," Jackal mockingly saluted the family as he turned and left abruptly without speaking to anyone else.

"What's that about?" Linda asked as the three made their way to the parking lot.

"I can't imagine," Phil said, shaking his head.

"It's a trick," Nicholas said confidently as they reached the car. Philip unlocked the doors by pressing the key fob, and everyone got in.

"What's he after?" Philip asked as they climbed got into their seats.

"I don't know, but nothing good," Nicholas said, shaking his head.

Over roast chicken, mashed potatoes, buttered corn, and fresh-baked rolls, the family talked casually. Jackal dug into the food, and Linda wondered if it was his first home-cooked meal in a while. After dinner, she offered everyone coffee or tea, but Jackal declined. Nicholas went to play basketball with his friends and strategically stayed out of the way so Jackal would speak more openly.

As the three moved into the family room and settled comfortably, Jackal said, "I appreciate your letting me open up like this about your son. Ricky is a good guy. He just doesn't always make the best decisions."

No kidding, Philip thought. *And one of them is sitting across from me.*

"Everyone makes mistakes, especially when they're young," Linda offered.

"That's right, and I've made my share too," Jackal said.

Philip refrained from rolling his eyes, realizing he was judging the teen on hearsay rather than facts.

"I wanted to let you know that he has borrowed money and gone into debt, but he was probably too embarrassed to tell you," Jackal said, carefully picking his words.

"Really?" Philip asked, wondering if this was true. Ricky had never mentioned owing anyone money, and he seemed to get by on his meager earnings. "Who did he borrow from, and how much does he owe?"

"Well," Jackal said smoothly, shifting a little in the overstuffed chair, "he actually borrowed about $500 over the past few months, not all at once, a little here and there. It might even be more over that, but I just stopped keeping track. I figured he would repay it at some point, but so far, he hasn't. And now he avoids me. I wanted to let you know in case you want to help him or something."

"You mean like talk to him about his debt?" Linda asked.

"Yeah, or maybe like pay it off so he can be free and start fresh with no debt," Jackal said.

"Do you have any receipts?" Philip asked.

"Not on me, but I could drop them off or email them if you want," he offered.

"Why don't you do that so I can talk to Ricky about it?" Philip asked.

"I can do that tonight or tomorrow," Jackal said. "I was wondering, though, if you would be able to pay me back the money he owes and then get it from him?"

Philip's mind raced. He had not expected this, and he wasn't sure it was true. On the other hand, if Jackal knew Ricky's family were Christians, he might expect a show of faith by their repaying the loan—if it existed.

"Why don't you send those receipts, and we'll take a look," Philip suggested. "When we see the dates and amounts, we might be able to figure out why Ricky was borrowing money at those times."

"Sure thing," Jackal said, getting up and offering his hand again.

Philip stood and took it with a firm shake. "Thanks for letting us know, Jack," he said.

"I figured you would want to hear about it. I would if it were my kid," he gave a half grin.

After he left, Philip and Linda discussed the debt and wondered whether to ask Ricky directly. They decided not to, as he probably would deny it either way. They would wait for the receipts.

*****

"What did you think?" Desiree Crawford asked with a smile as she and Mel, along with Marie and Bob, headed toward their cars parked near each other in the church parking lot.

Holding Bob's arm affectionately, Marie said, "It's a beautiful church, and the service was nice, just a little different from what we're used to."

"You've probably not seen that much emotional drama," Mel grinned. "Jumping, dancing, singing spontaneously. People just let the Holy Spirit move them however it works on each of them."

"I noticed that," Marie said thoughtfully. "Financially too, apparently, since they passed the offering basket a few times."

"Oh, don't mind that," Desiree said, brushing the air with her hand. "That's just for the folks who have plenty to give as the Spirit moves them."

"That's a relief," Bob said as Marie nudged his arm with hers. "The preacher said something about good works being the road to heaven. Is that the church's view on salvation?"

The two couples had reached their cars and stood by the doors, waiting to get in as they finished their conversation.

Mel said, "Well yeah, I mean, lazy folks or bad people shouldn't get into heaven, right? We want—I mean, God wants—just those who desire to serve and please him."

"True," Marie said thoughtfully, "but don't confession and repentance come first? I mean, someone has to pay for our sins. Isn't that why Jesus died on the cross?"

"Well," Desiree said cautiously, "our pastor doesn't dwell on the past. We look toward the future by changing ourselves and living the right way to earn God's love and acceptance."

Marie and Bob exchanged a quick look. "Okay. Thanks for explaining that," Marie said.

As Mel opened the car door for his wife, he said, "It was great having you two join us. I hope you'll come back next week."

"We'll see," Bob said as he unlocked their car doors. "I work a lot of weekends."

"Take care," Desiree waved as she unrolled the car window. "Call me if you have any questions or want to get together, Marie."

"I will," Marie called as she got into her seat. As Bob climbed behind the steering wheel on the driver's side and shut his door, she said, "Something's off about that church, don't you think? They hardly mentioned God or Jesus. The focus was on getting people to live right and reap the riches of being a Christian."

"Yeah, I noticed that," Bob said, pulling out of the parking lot. "I've never been a big churchgoer, but even to me, that sounds weird." He waited for the corner light to turn green and then continued driving. "But that part about being blessed with financial riches was interesting. It makes sense that God would reward good people."

*****

Nicholas walked with a brisk step down the corridor toward the campus learning center. Pulling open the door, he glanced toward the large roundtable where Amy usually sat, and there she was. As he entered the room, she looked up and gave a small wave, inviting him over as there were no other student appointments ahead of him.

"Hey," he said, sitting down across from her, admiring her clear brown skin and bright smile that warmed his heart.

"Good morning," she said. Glancing at the clock, she added, "You're early, but that's okay as the student before you was a no-show."

"Great," Nicholas said, pulling open his book bag and taking out the biology notebook with assignments along with the textbook.

For the next hour, they went over his upcoming biology report and the midterm exam that was just a few weeks away. Time passed quickly, and Nicholas was dismayed when Amy said, "I hope that answers your questions. Feeling more prepared for the report now?"

"Yeah, I guess so," Nicholas said. "Of course, I'll keep reviewing my notes while writing the paper."

"Let me know if you have questions," Amy said.

"I will," Nicholas replied, packing up his book bag. "By the way," he said slowly, unsure of his words, "would you like to maybe have coffee when your tutoring shift is over?"

Amy's look of surprise turned to one of pleasure. "Sure, I'd like that. Meet you at Campus Coffee at 4:00 p.m. if that works for you?"

"Perfect," Nicholas said, elated. "See you then."

He could hardly get through his classes waiting to see her "off duty" from tutoring. But he forced himself to pay attention and take good notes. At 4:00 p.m. sharp, he walked into the campus café and saw Amy sitting in a side booth. He ordered coffee and took the steaming cup to join her. She seemed relaxed and comfortable, and he soon felt that way too. Soon, two hours had passed as they talked about their families, the schools they had grown up attending, and social issues each had noticed recently.

"I don't know how much worse society can get with disrespecting the sanctity of life," Nicholas began when he noticed Amy's expression grow pale.

Looking down, she said, "I know. It's terrible. I feel awful."

"*You* feel awful? Why?" Nicholas asked.

She paused before answering. "I've only told a couple of people about this, but for some reason, I trust you," she said tentatively. "There's something about your personality and the way you were raised that makes me feel comfortable…and safe…around you. I don't know why."

Stunned, Nicholas waited for the slender girl to collect her thoughts and ease her way further into the conversation.

"Last year, when I started college, I got mixed up with the wrong person," she began. "It was a brief romance, and then I—I got pregnant."

"Oh," Nicholas said, taken aback. He had never thought about her having a child.

"Then, I had an abortion."

Shocked, Nicholas said nothing. He had known people who had had abortions in high school, but he had never known them personally. Now, face-to-face with Amy's confession, he wasn't sure what to say or even what he thought. He believed abortion was wrong; he had been taught that from the Bible and his parents. But he didn't know why Amy had told him or what to do about it. Silently he prayed, *Lord, please give me the right thoughts and words.*

"Amy, I'm sorry. It sounds like it was a difficult situation, and you made a hard choice." He paused, searching for more words. "I can only imagine the pain you must have gone through and what you still struggle with at times. Have you talked to God about it?"

There. He had said it, pointed her to God. He wasn't a good evangelist, but he felt the Lord had brought him to this conversation with a purpose.

She looked at him with an uncertain expression. "I tried, but it didn't work."

"What do you mean?" he asked.

"I tried praying, but it didn't feel like God was listening. I didn't get a sense that he replied."

"Well God doesn't talk to us in the same way we talk to each other. He communicates in other ways, like through the Bible or, sometimes, through friends and church or even circumstances. Do you ever read the Bible?"

"Not much," Amy admitted in a low voice. "Not for a long time. But my dad read Bible stories to me when I was a little girl."

"Would you like me to show you some passages that might help?" Nicholas asked softly, though no one was sitting near them.

"Yes," she said.

"My Bible is in the car. Can we sit outside on a bench near the pond?"

"Sure," she said, smiling. "It's really nice out there today."

They got up and went out to the car where Nicholas retrieved his Bible from the back seat. The pond was only a few minutes' walk away.

Opening his Bible as they took seats on a natural wood bench facing the pond where a small flock of geese was floating, Nicholas said, "Here's a verse that makes me feel better when I'm wrestling with something. It's Matthew 11:28. 'Come unto me, all ye that labor and are heavy laden, and I will give you rest.'"

He glanced up, and Amy appeared to be reflective. "That sounds nice," she murmured.

The pair continued to talk over the next hour as the golden October afternoon settled into a quiet evening.

*****

"Please help me!" An elderly woman called loudly as she tossed back and forth in her hospital bed. Linda rushed into the room to answer the patient's call light.

"What's wrong, Mrs. Bryden?"

"The pain—it's terrible! I can't stand this. Help me please," the woman moaned, gray hair matted on her pillow.

Checking the woman's chart, Linda saw that she wasn't due for her next pain medication for another hour. "You can have the next dose at four thirty," Linda said in a comforting tone.

Mrs. Bryden gasped. "I can't—can't wait that long. Help me please!"

Linda struggled in her spirit about what to do. There was only one thing she could offer, but she was forbidden by hospital rules from doing so. Praying silently, she asked, *Dear Father, please forgive me, but I feel you have put this woman in my care for a reason.*

Taking the feeble woman's hand in both of hers, Linda prayed aloud, "Dear God, please soothe Mrs. Bryden's pain. Help her to feel your presence and be at peace."

The woman's trembling slowed and then ceased. She looked at Linda with a relaxed expression, almost as if she had been given pain relief. "Thank you, my dear. The pain is less now. You must be an angel sent by God."

"You're welcome," Linda smiled, gently squeezing the woman's fingers before laying her hand back on the bedcover. She got up and left the room to continue her duties, not knowing whether the supervisor would find out and fire her and almost not caring. Although she and Philip counted on her income for their bills, some things were more important than a job. If she got fired, Linda would just have to tighten the budget even more, and she found that she

66

enjoyed doing that as it gave her greater control over their spending and was beginning to build their savings.

Sunday night, Phil sat in his study with the Bible open before him on the desk. Linda was working the second shift to attend church that morning since she was scheduled to work every other weekend at the hospital.

Poring over the Scriptures, Phil realized he needed to go deeper in the Word to find God's answers to pressing questions. Before reading, he bowed his head and prayed aloud: "Dear Lord, I praise you as our Creator and Savior. Thank you for all that you do to give us life and enable us to enjoy it. Guide me into truth so I can deal with things in ways that will bring honor to you. Amen." He turned to 2 Timothy chapter 3 and read aloud the first seven verses softly.

"But know this, that in the last days perilous times will come: For men will be lovers of themselves, lovers of money, boasters, proud, blasphemers, disobedient to parents, unthankful, unholy, unloving, unforgiving, slanderers, without self-control, brutal, despisers of good, traitors, headstrong, haughty, lovers of pleasure rather than lovers of God, having a form of godliness but denying its power. And from such people turn away! For of this sort are those who creep into households and make captives of gullible women loaded down with sins, led away by various lusts, always learning and never able to come to the knowledge of the truth."

Ricky came to mind—disobedient to parents, unthankful, and unholy. How Philip wished he could find a way to reach his son and make him hear and accept the truth. But he knew that each person has a choice, and Ricky had turned away from God. Hopefully, someone or something would bring him to the Lord before it was too late.

A quick memory came to mind of Marie's phone call that afternoon, describing their visit to the Crawfords' church. Some things she had said were disturbing, and he wondered if these verses he had just read would apply to that church's doctrine and teachings, "having a form of godliness but denying its power." He had warned his daughter to be careful and not get drawn into a church that taught anything but the saving power of Jesus Christ, crucified and risen, to pay for humanity's sins. Marie had agreed with him, but he wondered if she would be swayed. She and Bob were having financial problems with Bob's hours at work cut back. He would pray they did not fall into temptation or look for an easier route to salvation through wrong teachings.

CHAPTER 8

"Abel," Gloria Skinner called from the kitchen, "breakfast is ready. I want to see how you like this new blueberry muffin recipe. Low fat, low sugar, and low carb."

The reverend got up from his favorite chair in the family room where he watched the morning news feeds from not just the US, representing both the liberal and conservative perspectives so he could be fully aware of what was happening, but also news coverage from several foreign nations as well: Australia's *Sky News*; the UK's *Daily Mail* and *BBC*; *Al Arabiya*, the Saudi news station based in Dubai; and *The Jerusalem Post* among others. Abel Skinner felt that it was his duty as a pastor to know what was happening in the world and to steer his church flock through the midst of global tumult, using the Bible for navigation.

"Coming," he said, switching off the monitor and getting up. "If they're that healthy, I don't know how they can have any taste."

Gloria chuckled. She was cooking healthier meals, but Abel was not taking to them as well as she had hoped. Maybe in time, he would get used to eating foods with less fat, sugar, and salt.

Over breakfast, consisting of scrambled eggs and whole wheat toast with a glass of orange juice, Gloria saved the muffins for afterward with coffee. She happily noticed that her husband was eating the muffin without commenting on its taste.

"Do you like it?" she asked tentatively, finishing the last of hers and resisting the impulse to have another. She would freeze the rest.

"Hmm?" He looked up in surprise, and she realized in the last few moments, he had been lost in thought.

"The muffin—was it as bad as you thought it would be?"

"Oh no, it was fine. Tasted good."

Looking at his face, she said, "Okay, I can see something's bothering you. What is it?"

Reflecting momentarily, he replied, "The news just keeps getting worse. Every day there are new conflicts around the world with rumors that war is just about to break out or worsen somewhere, locusts in northern Africa, drought in the Middle East, and unprecedented monsoon flooding in India. I keep waiting for things to settle down, you know, as if the world is going through temporary changes. But things keep speeding up and getting worse. If I didn't know where this all was headed, I'd be worried."

Gloria sighed. "I know. Most people seem too busy with their daily lives to pay much attention to world events. My friend Katherine was saying the other day that we need to take notice of what's going on. The Lord is going to return one day right quick, and we'll be out of here. The unbelievers won't know what to think, and there won't be any Christians left to explain or advise them how to be saved."

Abel sat back, nodding. "I'm trying to get the congregation to take it seriously to believe that we truly are in the end-times as foretold in the Bible. Some of them think those prophecies are just allegories or figurative lessons to teach people how to live. They don't realize it's all literal, and it's starting to happen right before our eyes! In fact, it started several years ago when Israel was reborn as a modern nation in 1948 and even before that. But since then, things have been happening faster and faster."

"Oh yes," Gloria said, "the Bible says the end-times will unfold like a woman in labor. Do you remember when I had James?"

"I sure do," Abel nodded vigorously. "Neither of us got much rest for a couple of days. I was scared for you and the baby, worried how things would turn out. But I had to trust God, and he brought us all through."

"The pains started out slight. I thought it wasn't that bad. Maybe I'd be one of the strong ones that could give birth and hardly feel it."

Abel chuckled and shook his head. "Then do you recall how things progressed, or were you kind of out of it at that point?"

Gloria laughed. "I surely do recall those hours. It got worse. The pain was unbelievable—felt like my spine was going to snap. But all I could do was ask God for the strength to bear it."

"And you did, my love," Abel smiled, covering her hand on the table with his. "You came through it beautifully." He sat back and continued, "That's how the world is now. The pains have started, and they're revving up, getting worse every day. First, one part of the world and then another. I just hope our church family is prepared. I may offer to meet with each family in their homes like I did two years ago to offer comfort and reassurance along with hope."

"I think they'll appreciate that," Gloria said warmly, admiring, as she often did, her husband's faith and concern for his pastoral flock.

"One thing is especially troubling," he added as his features darkened in thought. "There's a new leader being acclaimed in Italy. Even the Pope endorses him. I think the government wants to make him the president or prime minister but with absolute power since their socialist government is failing. His name is Vittorio Russo. Vittorio means victor by the way. He's around fifty years old, attractive, well-liked by most, and he has been taking a middle position in politics, except that he envisions a new world order, a one-world government. I think he has an underlying superiority attitude that holds other people in contempt, though he tries not to show it."

"What happens if they elect him as president of Italy?" Gloria asked in concern as she folded her arms on the table.

"Bad things," Abel Skinner said gravely.

*****

True to his word, surprising Philip and Linda, Jackal emailed copies of alleged IOU receipts showing amounts borrowed by Ricky with what looked like his signature at the bottom of pieces of notebook paper. There were amounts of $40, $67, $75, $115, $128, and others progressing to more than $500 as Jackal had said. There was no pattern to the dates, with "loans" occurring every few weeks.

"What do you think?" Phil asked Linda after dinner when he showed her the attachments to Jackal's email on his computer. "Are these from Ricky?"

She scanned them intently, looking for handwriting clues to indicate the signatures had been forged. She knew Jackal could have somehow gotten hold of Ricky's signature on anything—a charge slip for gas, a fast-food purchase—and copied it in the receipts.

"I don't know," she said. "Maybe we should just pay Jackal and be done with it."

"But maybe that won't be the end," Phil said. "Maybe he'll keep sending more receipts."

"We'll let him know that this is the only time we will cover our son's debts. He will have to collect future loans on his own."

Phil was not happy about the situation, but he couldn't think of a better way to handle it. Work was frenzied in the accounting office, and as he studied Scripture more intently, he realized that it looked very much like the end-times shaping up. They needed to prepare and alert others, especially Ricky, along with Marie and Bob.

"All right. His email includes a mailing address. I'll send a check, and that'll be the end of it. But we need to discuss this with Ricky."

"I know," Linda said, "but even if he borrowed the money, he'll probably deny it."

"Well, we still have to tell him about it. If we're making a mistake in paying Jackal, then he will have to live with a guilty conscience."

"I hope his conscience is still working," Linda said heavily.

*****

Ricky's mobile phone beeped a text message while he was stocking shelves at the supermarket, the only job he had been able to get in a while. Glancing at the name, he clicked to answer after looking around to be sure his boss was nowhere around.

"What?" he hissed.

"Hey, man, take it easy. I got you some."

"I told you, Jackal, I don't want anymore. I'm done with that."

"What if I told you it was paid for?"

"Paid for? Who would buy me drugs?"

"You'd be surprised," Jackal giggled. "Come over and try this stuff. You won't believe it. You never have to retake it. You never have to talk to me again if you don't want to."

Ricky paused. He had been feeling awful since giving up drugs. His body ached, and his mind often went numb. He knew it took weeks or months to get back to anything like normal. But maybe a small dose of something would tide him over, just a little bit to finish things off.

Jackal seemed to read his thoughts or his silence. "My place when you get off work."

*****

Nicholas was able to raise his biology grade. And by midterms, he was pulling a B average.

"Thanks for your help, Amy," he said one afternoon as they left the tutoring center to grab a beverage and take a walk around campus.

She said softly as they headed toward the student union, "No, thank you, Nicholas. I can't tell you how much better I feel about myself and life in general since you started sharing the Bible with me. I still don't have all the answers to my questions, but I feel like I'm in a good place now and headed in the right direction."

"That's great! God's love can transcend anything that life throws at us. It doesn't give us the right to keep on sinning, but Jesus's death on the cross pays for our sins and removes our guilt."

"That's the part I'm still working on," she said slowly, looking up at him as they walked in the warm autumn sunshine. "I believe that Jesus did live on earth and that he taught people how to live. I'm starting to understand the death and resurrection part. I just can hardly believe he went through all that for me—for my wrongdoing and sins."

"I know! It's amazing—the most wonderful feeling in the world," Nicholas smiled. He wanted to put his arm around her shoulders but decided it was too soon. He didn't want her to think he was taking advantage of her vulnerable state of mind.

"There's a campus Bible study that starts next week. Would you like to come?" he asked.

"I might do that," she said thoughtfully.

They reached the student union and went indoors to get coffee for their afternoon walk.

The weeks passed quickly. Halloween loomed, but church members took a casual approach to the holiday by letting kids trick-or-treat in innocent colorful costumes that did not glorify Satan or evil entities. No one suspected that a series of unique events with global impact would erupt to change the course of human history in a few days.

The following Tuesday, news headlines around the world screamed, "Vittorio Russo, elected president of Italy!" Adriano Alba was elected as prime minister and president of the council of ministers who functioned as the executive committee to Italy's central government. The two leaders had worked together in Italy's government for decades to reinforce socialist values and break the traditional bond between religious and secular forces. Renowned for his allegedly peacemaking strategies, Russo was acclaimed as a welcome figure to deal with Italy's scandal-laced government and struggling economy while maintaining the status quo.

Reading the headlines on that chilly November morning from his family room chair, Abel Kinner was concerned. He had a bad feeling about Vittorio Russo. Was he the one whose coming had been foretold for centuries, with Alba as his attending second-in-command? Abel pulled open his Bible to prepare for Sunday's sermon, continuing his series on the end-times. Having moved through the Matthew passages of Jesus's teaching on this topic, Reverend Skinner was now arranging sermons based on Mark 13:5–13. He took copious notes as he read and reread the passage while consulting Bible commentaries piled on his desk.

> *And Jesus, answering them, began to say: "Take heed that no one deceives you. For many will come in My name, saying, 'I am He,' and*

will deceive many. But when you hear of wars and rumors of wars, do not be troubled; for such things must happen, but the end is not yet. For nation will rise against nation, and kingdom against kingdom. And there will be earthquakes in various places, and there will be famines and troubles. These are the beginnings of sorrows.

"But watch out for yourselves, for they will deliver you up to councils, and you will be beaten in the synagogues. You will be brought before rulers and kings for My sake, for a testimony to them. And the gospel must first be preached to all the nations. But when they arrest you and deliver you up, do not worry beforehand, or premeditate what you will speak. But whatever is given you in that hour, speak that; for it is not you who speak, but the Holy Spirit. Now brother will betray brother to death, and a father his child; and children will revolt against parents and cause them to be put to death. And you will be hated by all for My name's sake. But he who endures to the end shall be saved."

Yes, he thought, looking up, *it is coming.*

He had been reading lately about this Vittorio Russo. In fact, Abel had ordered a newly published biography of the man who was fast becoming a European cultural icon as well as an influential leader with expansive influence. Long a proponent of separating church from state policies, Russo appeared to be on a mission to replace Italy's population of dedicated church followers with obedient government supporters. Although he did not personally agree with Catholic doctrine, Reverend Skinner respected the church's pro-life position and its conservative policies in related areas of family life. But it appeared that this Vittorio Russo was determined to sweep aside any remaining Christian influence to reinforce Italy's culture as forcefully secular with an autocratic government.

Although the US population, in general, paid little attention to European politics or culture, this turn of events would undoubtedly have tsunami ramifications that would eventually reach American shores. Italy was not the capital of Europe, but it had been the seat of Roman Catholicism for centuries. And although that influence had largely faded, the church still connected many countries and people throughout Europe and beyond. As the last bastions of the church fell in tandem with the persecution of evangelical Christians in various nations throughout the world, there would be no organized faith-based structure to protect people from the powerful one-world government that was being formed right in front of them if they took time to notice. It was well known that Russo had formed ties with world leaders in Canada, Hungary, and Turkey, among others, to forge a new global government with a new currency and widespread surveillance. Russo spoke of establishing a truth-and-justice department, similar to the one operating in South Africa, to rectify the wrongs of the past by eliciting apologies from previous government leaders who had "harmed" their nations and people with wrong or illicit actions. With justice meted out, punishments issued, and restitution paid, the new one-world government could proclaim an era of peace and security for all. When Europe embraced the new model, the United States and other Western nations would have little recourse but to follow suit or be cut off from global resources and networks that were financially necessary for a healthy economy.

It's like a domino effect, Reverend Skinner thought soberly. *Now that it has begun with this man becoming the president of Italy, things will move even more rapidly to bring about the end of days. I know I'm right about a pretribulation rapture. If so, we won't be here for long.*

*****

"No answer yet," Phil said in response to the question on Linda's face. "I don't know where he goes all the time, but I'm sure he's not working sixty hours a week."

"I wish he were," Linda said. "Maybe that would keep Ricky out of trouble. Did you text him?"

"Yeah," Phil said, setting his phone down on the coffee table. "Twice, asking him to call. Nothing yet."

"Let's pray," Linda suggested.

*****

Ricky slumped against the back of Jackal's brown sofa, ignoring his phone's text beep, trying to stay awake. His brain was fuzzy and wouldn't cooperate. It felt wonderful, like he was floating, free without restraint, being lifted into the air, and borne aloft by a gentle breeze that seemed to caress him as he moved through clouds of soft pastel colors. Was it sunrise or sunset? He could not tell, and it didn't matter, except someone kept bothering him with questions.

"Ricky, hey, man, wake up just for a second. Then I've got some more stuff for you. You're a beneficiary on your pop's insurance policy, right? You and your sister and brother, just the three of you? I mean if your mom wasn't around."

Ricky tried to speak, but his mouth felt as fuzzy as his brain. A dim spark of thought wondered why Jackal was asking about his dad's life insurance. *Dad was fine, healthy. No reason to ask...*

"C'mon, Ricky. No strings, just you and the sibs get everything if something happens to your old man—I mean, your dad and mom—right?"

Ricky tried to push out a few words, but they huddled in his throat as though fearful of exiting his mouth. Darkness swirled as his eyes rolled back, and he was pushed forcefully into the gaping darkness that engulfed both body and mind as Jackal jostled his shoulder to bring him back to the light.

CHAPTER 9

"*Buongiorno*, Adriano," Vittorio Russo smiled blandly and motioned his long-time partner into the conference room before closing the door. Although the new president of Italy spoke English in business meetings, he would include occasional Italian phrases as a personal touch with Italian cronies.

"Good morning, Vittorio. How are you adjusting to your new position?" Adriano beamed as he took a seat and opened his brief-case. Settling documents on the long mahogany table, he waited politely for a reply.

"Perfectly," Vittorio said, coming to sit down across from Adriano. "You received the agenda I sent last week?"

"Of course," Adriano said, tapping a file he'd placed on the table, "and the unofficial agenda as well."

Both men laughed.

"So you'll attend the global economic revival with me in December?" Vittorio asked.

"I wouldn't miss it," Adriano said, opening the file of documents he had collected on the global economy. Pulling out a map, he handed it to the president. "I've put the finishing touches on your economic reset plan. I think the GER will go for it."

Vittorio placed his hands behind his head, nodding. "A few won't, but we can get it passed without full support."

"What about the world economic forum in January when you challenge the leadership?" Adriano asked. "You're new to running to the nation. Will they advance you to the role of global director?"

"We have a few months to lay the foundation. It may take longer, but we have our ways, some less well-known than others," he said calmly.

"Ah, yes," Adriano brightened. "We have, shall we say, supernatural aid at our fingertips when needed."

"Indeed," Vittorio said intently. "The foundation is in place, and the plan is nearly ready. When the first domino falls in December, everything will follow in rapid succession to challenge the pomp and popularity of Christmas this year."

"Most people will choose money over religion any day," Adriano agreed.

They set to work on the charts and forms that Adriano had settled on the large table in the elegantly furnished meeting room.

*****

"I need more time," Amy said to Nicholas on the phone. "It sounds great, but I'm not ready for a Bible study."

Nicholas said, "It's not really a Bible study, Amy, it's more of a casual gathering for people who are interested in learning more about Christians and the Bible."

The phone was quiet for a moment. Then Amy said, "I'm sorry, Nicholas, it's not for me right now. I have to take care of some other things."

After saying their goodbyes, Nicholas lay down on his bed and tucked a pillow under his neck, wondering why Amy didn't want to come to the campus Christian group. He had a feeling it might have something to do with a football team player, Quentin, who had been coming to see Amy for biology tutoring as the class was needed for his physical therapy major. Nicholas had seen him in the study center two or three times, either before or after his appointments with Amy. And she had seemed more preoccupied—almost distant—with him over the past couple of weeks. Now that the weather was turning colder leading up to Thanksgiving, they couldn't walk outdoors as much, and Nicholas wasn't quite ready to bring her home to meet his parents yet. Nor did he think it was a good idea to hang out in her dorm room. Their friendship that had begun on solid ground began to slowly disintegrate. Nicholas was mature enough to understand this as a natural progression of events. You got to know someone for a couple of months, and if your personalities click, you would start going out more regularly. He had thought that he and Amy were headed in that direction, but lately, he had noticed subtle changes in her and understood what was happening. Although disappointed, Nicholas would continue praying for Amy to develop a stronger interest in Jesus and find a friend, if not him, who would invite her to church or share the Bible with her.

Thanks, Lord, he prayed silently, grateful for direction. He didn't necessarily need to be seeing someone right now as schoolwork kept him busy, and he played basketball with his friends. But his ego was slightly bruised. He would get over it.

Maybe he should check on his brother. Pressing the recorded number, he waited while it buzzed several times—three, four. On the fifth ring, his brother's voice said in a cranky tone, "What d'ya want?"

"Hey, bro, nice to talk to you too. Whassup?"

"Same ole. You?"

"Same. Wanna get somethin' to eat? I'll buy."

There was a pause. *Man*, Nicholas thought, *what's with all these pauses people are giving me? I gotta find more appreciative friends.*

"Taco Joe's, twenty minutes," Ricky said as if doing his brother a favor.

"Gotcha," Nicholas agreed.

Over a platter of tacos, the brothers talked little, though Nicholas tried to keep the conversation going. He was dismayed to see Ricky looking so tired and old for his twenty-five years.

"Everything okay?" he asked casually while stuffing shredded lettuce into a taco shell with diced chicken, chopped tomatoes, and green onions.

"Dandy," Ricky snarled in a surly tone.

"Do you need anything?" Nicholas offered tentatively.

Ricky's eyes blazed. "Yeah, I need punks like you to stay out of my life and quit bothering me." He looked down and shook his head in irritation and then tried to put together the remains of his taco that had sprawled all over his plate.

"You know," Nicholas began, "you can find answers to the hard questions in the Bible. God loves you, Ricky. He loves all of us. He wants a relationship with you. Why don't you just pray to him, talk to him?"

Ricky's lips tightened as his eyes narrowed, trying not to reveal the withdrawal symptoms he was struggling with physically and emotionally. "Yeah, I know. He loves me so much that he put me in a family with parents that preach religion nonstop and try to turn me into a model citizen like them or you," he added in disgust. He slid his trembling hands into his lap so Nicholas wouldn't notice.

They ate in silence for a couple of minutes before Nicholas asked, "Do you keep up with the news? A lot is happening in the world right now. I think we're headed for trouble."

"I got troubles of my own. Money, relationships, job. I don't care 'bout no world troubles if that's what you mean."

Nicholas tried to think of any way he could help his brother. "Ricky," he said quietly, although no one was sitting near their booth, "Jesus is going to rapture the Christians soon. It could be anytime. The world is getting worse each day, just like in the days of Noah or Lot. Things are bad. Look around, and you'll see it everywhere. No respect for life, for family, for the elderly, or the sick. People will do anything for self-gratification like steal, lie, kill, destroy. We have to be ready to leave in an instant!"

Ricky snickered. "You sound like a bad rerun from *The Twilight Zone*. Give it up, Nicholas. I know that you base your life on Christianity, but it's not for me."

"Then what is for you?" Nicholas asked curtly, surprising himself by the sharp tone. This was the second rejection of Christianity he had gotten today, and he wasn't taking it lightly.

"Just leave me alone," Ricky said tightly. "I gotta go." He started to scoot out of the booth.

"Wait," Nicholas said, putting a hand on his arm. "Mom and Dad love you, and so do I. We're worried about you. Come home for a while. Get some rest. We'll help you figure things out."

"Get out of my face, punk," Ricky said, jerking his arm away. "See ya…or not." He left abruptly.

Dear Father, please help my brother, Nicholas prayed silently, sadly watching his brother's departure.

*****

Marie left her spinning class sweaty but exhilarated. It had been a great workout, and she felt reenergized after a busy workday. Driving home, she got a text from Desiree.

"Hey, Marie, hope you're having a great day! Truth Temple is hosting a visitors' get-together this week after the service. Would you and Bob like to come?"

Pressure, Marie thought. *Just what I don't need.* "I'll check with Bob and get back to you," she texted back, hoping his limited interest in the church would squelch future participation.

"Why not, honey?" he asked over the roast chicken and jojos she brought home from the supermarket for dinner. "We might benefit from their church's prosperity message," he joked.

"C'mon, Bob. You know that's all smoke and mirrors," Marie said.

"Let's give it another try," he suggested. "Besides, they'll have refreshments, so we can stay in our grocery budget this week."

"You never stop with the laughs, do you?" she said good-naturedly. "Okay, we'll go this once, but then we can tell them it's not for us."

"Right," he said, biting into a deep-fried chicken leg.

They felt compelled to attend the Sunday morning church service first. Afterward, they gathered with four other couples and the pastor to discuss church doctrine and membership requirements.

"We're very open here," Pastor Williams said affably. Looking around the circle of visitors who were politely listening to his explanation of the church mission and goals, he added, "We welcome anyone who wants to worship with us, no questions asked. If they behave themselves, they can join us for service, volunteer in ministry, and serve in various capacities."

"Do we need to take membership classes first?" Doreen Watkins asked.

"That's what this is," Pastor Williams grinned. "If you are thinking about becoming a member, we'll ask you to attend one more group meeting like this, and then we'll take a church vote to confirm you as a new member after the following Sunday service."

"Are background checks required to work with the children or youth?" Dave Belmont asked as his wife nodded.

"No," the pastor shook his head. "We operate on the honor system. When you offer to volunteer, we trust you to care for others according to biblical principles."

"What about tithes?" Lester Crewes asked. "Is a certain amount, like 10 percent of your income, required?"

"We believe tithing represents your trust in God. We believe everything belongs to God, and the tithe represents how we give back to him." The apostle Paul taught we should give as we want the Lord to bless us. Members give whatever the Holy Spirit moves them to give."

After the meeting, Marie and Bob talked over what they had learned as they drove home.

"Everyone seems nice," Marie said thoughtfully. "The church seems to accept everyone without limiting people who are struggling with sin or race or disabilities or anything."

"Definitely a plus," Bob said, heading to their bedroom to change out of his church clothes when they got home.

That week, they talked more about becoming members of Truth Temple.

"We really should belong to a church," Marie told Bob one morning as they got ready for work.

"Yeah, it wouldn't hurt," Bob agreed.

They decided to attend the second membership meeting. It went smoothly and confirmed the couple's positive impression, so they committed to joining the church. Bob convinced Marie they should start putting more money in the offering plate, comparing it to "sowing seeds of wealth," he explained.

"I very much doubt we're going to get wealthy," Marie countered. "But maybe we will be well-off in heaven."

"I'll take mine here," Bob snorted as they eased through the fast-food drive-through lane after the Sunday service.

*****

Philip missed having Linda at home on the evenings she worked at the hospital. Settling into his family room recliner, he switched on the news channel and clicked through one station after another to hear the latest updates. From a Christian perspective, current events were deeply troubling. The first channel's news anchor was interviewing delighted parents in a New England public library where transgender persons in flashy cosmetics and wigs, as well as flamboyant dresses, were hosting *Story Hour* for elementary school students by reading aloud a book about a little boy who decided he wanted to become a girl.

Clicking to the next news channel, Phil listened as the news program cohosts announced the new state law that would allow aborted babies that survived and were born alive to be killed by medical staff. No specific method was mentioned, but Phil suspected any murder option would be legally permitted—choking, strangling, drowning, poisoning, and withholding food and water or medical care. He had heard about such things being done already in some abortion clinics, although the law up to this point did not officially condone the murder of a newborn. That was changing now with the new law being passed.

Unwilling to hear more terrible news around the nation, Philip switched to an international news station. The first channel satellite linked to a reporter in Nigeria who was standing near a church where dozens of residents were weeping and mourning. He reported that over seventy Christian church members had been rounded up and shot by a Muslim extremist group. Philip waited for the next international news story with a heavy heart, which was also disheartening: Chinese government officials had closed hundreds of churches throughout the country and threatened to expel or imprison anyone who claimed to be a Christian. In the news story that followed, European heads of state were praising the efforts of President Vittorio Russo to impose a universal basic income on Italy's economy in a model that was sure to gain popularity throughout the Western world. Already, President Russo was being hailed by the liberal media as the "savior" of the global economy that had been teetering on the verge of collapse. The man's fame was skyrocketing. Philip had never heard of a national leader rising to power and popularity so quickly, and it made him uneasy. There was something about President Russo's calm assurance that made the hair on the back of his neck stand up as if the man had unseen powers that would carry out his every wish.

Clicking to another channel, a news report indicated that more rocket attacks had been launched on Southern Israel and Northern Israel in recent hours. The prime minister was holding an urgent meeting with the cabinet and the country's military leaders to determine the most effective response. In the next segment of the program, it was reported the recent Bosporus flare-ups of violence were turning deadlier as outside forces were joining both sides in escalating the conflict. Protests, skirmishes, and violent outbreaks against authority were occurring at an unprecedented rate around the globe.

"Has the world gone crazy?" Phil wondered aloud.

Disgusted, Phil clicked on one more channel. The first was making an emergency announcement with a red banner highlighting the event scrolling across the top of the screen: "Greece has experienced a third aftershock of magnitude 6.4 following the devastating 8.5-magnitude quake that shook the region earlier today. Survivors are being pulled from the rubble of toppled buildings that include some well-known historical sites. Residents claim neither they nor older relatives can remember an earthquake of this size hitting the area in modern times."

Disturbed, Philip silently prayed for lives to be spared as the following story appeared: "A catastrophic earthquake estimated at a magnitude of 9.1 has just been reported in Cyprus and surrounding areas. News agencies are waiting for damage and fatality estimates. A preliminary geological team arriving on scene believes this may be related to the 8.5 earthquakes that shook Greece a short time ago."

What is going on? he wondered.

He clicked through two more channels that appeared to be showing raw footage of the earthquake damage before pausing at the subsequent news station: "Seismologists are warning that Yellowstone Park may be at elevated risk for a major earthquake eruption from the volcanic super caldera that has been bubbling toward the surface of the lake for the past three years. Geologists are converging to evaluate and monitor the situation."

Wow! If the Yellowstone super caldera blows, our country is in huge trouble! Philip took a deep breath to steady his thoughts and sat back in his chair. What did all these earthquakes so close together mean? Could it be the birth pains of the end-times were increasing in strength and frequency? He fervently hoped other people—especially unbelievers—were feeling the same sense of dread that he was experiencing so they could turn to Jesus and be saved.

Clicking off the television, Phil put down the remote control and thought about what he had just heard. Reaching for his Bible, he opened it and thumbed through the New Testament to read the sections suggested by Reverend Skinner the previous Sunday.

"All right," he said aloud to himself, "here we are in Luke 21:10–18." He read the passage aloud to hear it as well as see it. "'Then He said to them, "Nation will rise against nation, and kingdom against kingdom. And there will be great earthquakes in various places, and famines and pestilences; and there will be fearful sights and great signs from heaven. But before all these things, they will lay their hands on you and persecute *you,* delivering *you* up to the synagogues and prisons. You will be brought before kings and rulers for My name's sake. But it will turn out for you as an occasion for testimony. Therefore settle *it* in your hearts not to meditate beforehand on what you will answer; for I will give you a mouth and wisdom which all your adversaries will not be able to contradict or resist. You will be betrayed even by parents and brothers, relatives and friends; and they will put *some* of you to death. And you will be hated by all for My name's sake. But not a hair of your head shall be lost. By your patience possess your souls."'"

It's all there—Christian persecution, nation against nation, "great" earthquakes. And we have been hearing about famines and pestilences for a while now. Some believers will end up in prison for the Lord's sake, but it will be an opportunity to share our faith with unbelievers. And God will give us the right words when they are needed.

CHAPTER 10

Switching off the television late-night news, Reverend Abel Skinner stood up and stretched. "Things are looking pretty bad," he remarked to Gloria, who was crocheting a child-size afghan with pastel shades of yarn in a traditional design.

"And that's all to the good as far as Christians are concerned," she said with a smile. "Of course, we don't want to see anyone suffer or miss out on heaven. But all these terrible world events are likely going to catch some people's attention, and maybe they will get saved."

"I sure hope so, but a lot of folks are going to be struggling as we get further into the end-times. What are you making?"

"It's a gift for a new member of the church, a single mom. The ladies are giving her a baby shower."

"Well, it looks really nice. You are truly an artist, my dear."

"Thank you, Abel. I love it when you sweet-talk me," Gloria giggled.

He bent over and kissed the top of her head. "Speaking of church, did you notice that young man sitting in the back last Sunday? I tried to catch him before he left, but he rushed out after talking to the Bullock family."

"I did notice him, but I don't know who he is. Do you?"

Abel straightened and thought for a second before saying, "I believe he's a friend of Ricky, Phil and Linda's oldest son. He's probably one of the reasons Ricky has stopped coming to church."

"Really?" Gloria asked, deftly pulling stitches along the side of the blanket. "Ricky is old enough to make his own decisions, don't you think?"

"That's true. But that teenager is allegedly running a local gang that's into drugs and committing all kinds of crimes to support their addiction. I understand that Ricky joined willingly, and that's why we've asked Brother Phil to temporarily step down from the deaconship. But this gang leader, not sure of his name, uses drugs and blackmail to recruit members and keep them in bondage."

"Well," Gloria said, glancing up while her fingers kept rhythmically stitching the baby afghan that was slowly coming together in her lap, "let's pray for all of them. These young people today have many temptations that we didn't have to deal with at their age."

"Maybe so," the reverend said. He sat down on the other end of the sofa and reached for his wife's hand. She laid down her crochet needle and clasped his fingers.

"Dear God, please help our young people to turn their thoughts to you. Bring something or someone into their lives to show them the error of their ways and get them to confess their sins and repent before you. Give us the wisdom to know how to respond according to your will. In Jesus's name. Amen."

"Amen," Gloria echoed, squeezing her husband's hand before taking up her crochet hook again.

"Do you need anything before I head upstairs for the night?" Abel asked.

"No, hon, but thanks for asking. I'll be up shortly. Get some good rest."

"You too, my dear."

*****

As the November evening settled into chilly dusk, Jackal stood in a vacant lot on the outskirts of town. The lot was overgrown with weeds and littered with debris, but the nearest house was several blocks away, and there were no lights on. The lanky youth lined up in a row on a broken-down picnic table several empty food cans that he'd fished out of a dumpster near his house in the projects. Pulling the gun that Ricky had given him from the hoodie pouch, he checked to be sure it was loaded. Jackal didn't have much experience with handguns, but he'd looked up some basic usage instructions online and was now going to do target practice. He needed to be an expert shot for the job he was lining up.

He hadn't figured out how to use a silencer on the gun, so he looked around in all directions before taking aim at the first can. *Bang!* The bullet missed and disappeared in the tall weeds beyond.

Swearing aloud, he tried to recall what he had read online. Pulling his right hand up to the recommended position, he stared at the end can sitting on the wooden table, aimed steadily, and fired. *Whiz!* The bullet nicked the can but kept going.

Progress, Jackal thought. Aiming once more, he waited an extra second to keep the target can in sight before pulling the trigger. *Bing!* The can shot backward and disappeared in the tall grass.

"Yeah," Jackal smirked. He spent the next twenty minutes repeating the moves with each can until he had hit every one of them into the weeds. He wanted to back up and try shooting from a greater distance but decided it was too dark. Tomorrow he would be back.

*****

When Nicholas got home, he almost told his dad about meeting Ricky but decided against it. There was nothing good to say, and he didn't want to upset his parents any further than they already were about their older son.

After changing into his workout clothes for basketball practice, he paused by the family room where Phil sat with the Bible on his lap, looking contemplative.

"Hey, Dad, how was your day?"

"Oh, it was okay, Nick. How about yours?" Phil was proud of his younger son who was everything parents wanted their child to be: thoughtful, responsible, and most of all, committed to a relationship with God.

"It was so-so. Nothing terrible or wonderful," he grinned.

"Nice way to put it, son. Are you heading out for practice?" Phil asked.

"Yeah, I'll be home around ten. No homework tonight—a nice change of pace!" he added.

"Enjoy the workout."

"I will, Dad, g'night."

Phil wondered if the events that were starting to shake the world would reach their family. Then he realized it wasn't a matter of "if" but "when". Part of him felt sad and nostalgic for the mostly good life their family had enjoyed until now. But another part—a growing awareness—thrilled to the prospect of meeting Jesus face-to-face soon. If only Ricky and Marie would find their way to the Lord. He would keep praying for that, joined by Linda, Nicholas, their friends, and church family, as well as praying for the loved ones of others who, if they did not repent, risked facing the horrors of the coming tribulation as well as eternal exile from God.

As Linda made evening rounds to each patient under her care, she paused by the bedside of seventy-eight-year-old Harold Lyons who had suffered a major heart attack a week ago and had just come to her floor from ICU. Taking his vital signs and recording them in his chart, her heart grew tender as the shadows lengthened over his face, and his breathing grew shallower. Although the signs were not severe enough to warrant calling a code that would bring emergency medical staff on the run, she recognized the shadows of death extending over his frail form. She wanted to save him but didn't know how. He was in poor health, and there was a do-not-resuscitate order on the door to his room and above his bed. Linda didn't know if he had requested the DNR order or if the family had requested it, but there was no turning back now unless Mr. Lyons asked the order to be changed, and that was not likely.

Dear Lord, I don't know this man's heart, but you do. Please save him, even now, if he has not already accepted Jesus as his Savior. Give him comfort and ease his passing and guide me to do your will.

Abruptly, Mr. Lyons opened his eyes and looked around, appearing dazed.

"I'm Linda, your nurse," she said, laying her hand on his and leaning toward him so he could see her face. As his eyes focused, he smiled. "Y-yes, Linda, he told me you would be here."

"The doctor?" Linda asked softly.

"No," Mr. Lyons said faintly, "Someone up there." He glanced toward the ceiling. "He said to find you, and you would help me."

A chill ran down Linda's back. Was it possible that he had been told that from above?

"I am here to help, Mr. Lyons. What can I do to make you more comfortable?"

"No, no, it's…it's about the other. My…my soul. I'm not ready. Please help me."

Linda's heart fluttered. The director of nursing had explicitly told her not to proselytize any patients. But this dying elderly man was asking for spiritual support. And Linda had just prayed, seeking guidance from the Lord.

Taking his hand in hers, she said gently, "Let's pray, and you can tell the Lord what's on your heart. He is waiting to accept you. Just confess your sins and ask forgiveness."

He gasped and then sputtered, wheezing a little as he tried to whisper his words. Linda's eyes flew to the monitors he was hooked up to, but the numbers were not low enough to summon medical assistance. Even if she did, the staff would only provide palliative care rather than try to save his life.

"Dear God… Father…help me…please. I-I'm sorry for the bad things I did. I walked out on my wife and kids. I cheated on some of my customers a long time ago. I'm so sorry. Please forgive me." His hand squeezed hers as tightly as he could manage, and she held his firmly.

After a second or two, his grip relaxed as a smile played at the corners of his mouth. The dark shadows did not recede. "Th-thank you, Lord. My Savior and…my God…."

His breathing ebbed and stopped. The monitor went flatline. The alarm sounded as Linda turned on his call light. The resident doctor darted into the room and took in the situation at a glance.

"Is he gone?" the young medic asked with a professional, rather than compassionate, air.

Nodding, Linda said, "Yes, it was peaceful."

"Good." The doctor took Mr. Lyons's vital signs and confirmed to the nurse who had followed him into the room, then added to her, "Call his family."

"They live in Chicago," the nurse said. "I tried reaching them earlier when his condition began to deteriorate, but they haven't called back yet. I just asked them to call here. I didn't say why."

"Okay, well try again. We'll keep him in the room for a little while in case some of the relatives live nearby and want to say goodbye."

The nurse left the room, and the doctor looked at Linda. "Are you all right?"

"Yes, I've cared for dying patients before," she said it politely as reassurance.

"You look so ethereal, almost otherworldly. Probably tired, aren't you?"

"A little," she admitted, "but I'm fine."

The doctor left to dictate the patient report, and Linda turned off the monitors and then stood beside the bed a few minutes more, not wanting to leave Mr. Lyons alone even though he was no longer actually there. She felt tears gathering in her eyes. *Thank you, Lord.*

"Linda?" a female voice said from the door of the room.

"Yes," she responded, startled. It was the director of nursing who was never in the hospital on an evening shift. Momentarily, Linda wondered if the DON was there to watch her.

"Would you step out here for a moment, please?" the woman's tone was icy. At least she showed respect for the deceased by confronting Linda in the hallway.

Joining her in the empty, quiet corridor, Linda waited for the gavel to fall.

"I couldn't help but overhear your conversation with Mr. Lyons. You talked about God with him, didn't you?"

"Yes, he asked me to," Linda said evenly.

"Do you recall our previous conversation on this subject?" The DON sounded like a principal correcting a schoolchild.

"Of course," Linda said. "I haven't been having these conversations with my patients. But Mr. Lyons was dying, and he specifically asked me—"

"To what? Prepare him for the afterlife? Why didn't you call another team member if he seemed agitated? They could have given him a sedative."

"There was no need," Linda said calmly. "He asked for me by name, and I granted his request."

Silence prevailed for several seconds as the DON stared at Linda's face, reading her expression. Finally, she spoke in a low voice to ensure no one could overhear, although it was unlikely with the patients sleeping and the nurses at the main floor station.

"I've been patient, and you were given another opportunity to follow the protocols. But you have not done so, not consistently. Linda, I'm going to have to place you on unpaid leave for a few weeks until we set up employee counseling for you. Come by my office tomorrow morning, and I'll have the paperwork ready."

Stunned, Linda watched as her supervisor headed down the hall. Without her paycheck, the family budget would be strained. She hoped there was enough in their new savings account to carry them through until she was working again. *If* she would be able to work here again. She had always tried to put the Lord first in her life, but now more than ever in recent days, the other areas of her life seemed to suffer for it. It did not matter. Linda's faith was most important. She believed in following the hospital rules, but no hospital rule trumped God's authority over the souls of the spiritually needy when it came to life and death.

They would make ends meet somehow. She remembered a verse she had memorized in her women's Bible study last year: "God *is* our refuge and strength, a very present help in trouble," she whispered aloud, "Psalm 46:1." Refreshed and strengthened, Linda resumed her duties to complete what would be her final shift for some time.

*****

Ricky rolled over on the sagging plaid couch that reeked of vomit and food waste and fell onto the floor. Dizzy, he pulled himself to a sitting position and stared around at the darkness. Through a window with sagging curtains, he could see the glare of the housing project's streetlights shining in the darkness. Then he remembered he had crashed at Jackal's place after losing his job and getting evicted for not paying rent. He had never kept his own place for long for these same reasons. Before, he had gone to an inner-city homeless shelter for a night or two, but the bleakness and shame of it had driven him to find another job and keep trying to support himself.

Now he had just about reached rock bottom. He couldn't seem to hold a supermarket job stocking shelves for more than a couple of weeks. Even when sober, he would get depressed and just want to sleep. Then Jackal would somehow find him, and the shameful routine would start over again. He could not count how many cycles he had been through. There had been a short time when Reverend Skinner had given him a part-time job cleaning the church on weekends along with a back room to sleep in until he could save money for an apartment. It was understood that Ricky would look for a better job. This was a "placeholder" so he could earn money for food and save the rest for a place to live and to use public transport.

While staying in the plain but clean small room at the back of the sanctuary that held a single bed, a desk, and chair, along with a countertop with a microwave oven, Ricky fumed at the position he found himself in—serving the church he'd grown up to despise. He hated his parents for the life he now lived—homeless, jobless, fading health, and few prospects. But he refused to be held accountable for his choices and instead blamed his parents for "not raising him right" and depriving him of basic living necessities. Jackal had taught him these catchphrases for when anyone questioned him about his family or present circumstances.

Now sitting on the dirty rug in Jackal's mother's low-income apartment, he was glad he didn't have to deal with Jackal's parents as well as his own. His mother had her own drug habit that she shared with her current boyfriend at his apartment in an adjoining neighborhood that wasn't much better than the housing development. It was just Ricky and Jackal here mostly, with Jackal's little thirteen-year-old brother coming and going for food or drugs when needed.

Surrounded by mess and grime, Ricky remembered his clean bedroom at home. He thought of the home-cooked meals his mom had made and the times they had all sat in the family room watching funny movies and inspirational programs. Somehow he had come to find it all boring. As he came of age after barely graduating high school, Ricky had managed to get a trainee position at the local match factory. It wasn't exciting, but it paid the bills, and the work offered a future. But then he ran into Jackal after dropping off an employee whose driver's license had been suspended. The neighborhood had seemed shady, and Ricky didn't want to hang around after his coworker got out of the car, but a teen, about his age, walked over to the driver's side and asked Ricky if he had an extra cigarette.

"No, man, I don't smoke," Ricky said, starting to roll up the window.

"I got somethin' better than tobacco," Jackal had said knowingly.

That was the start of things. Ricky was soon addicted and experimenting with a variety of substances. He lasted another month in the factory's training position before he was let go for excessive absenteeism. He and Jackal became partners in an uneven but practical venture where Ricky brought money and goods to Jackal in exchange for weed, MDMA, cocaine, meth, and whatever drugs or alcohol Ricky asked.

Jackal held up his end with no problem, but Ricky found it harder and harder to keep working for money to buy what Jackal offered. With keen insight into human nature developed during his rough childhood and bad choices, Jackal saw Ricky's happening, which prompted him to begin working on plan B.

CHAPTER 11

"Did you check with the bank for the wire transfer?" Vittorio spoke into his cell phone while riding in the back seat of his late-model Ferrari as the driver navigated through busy morning Rome traffic.

"It arrived yesterday afternoon," Adriano's voice could be heard through the receiver.

"Good. Transfer it into the global economic revival account," Vittorio said. "We want to make a strong showing at the December summit."

"I'll take care of it this morning. Things are moving fast, President Russo."

Vittorio smiled at the use of his formal title by his close friend and associate. "That is the plan, which, as you know, was set in place long ago. A few more weeks or a couple of months at most, and everything will be in order. What did the Israeli PM say to the request for a meeting to discuss peace and security issues?"

"He wants to talk to you directly by phone first, then he may be willing to set up a personal meeting either here or in Jerusalem in the next week or so."

"Great. Set up the call and text me the details. Everything is proceeding on schedule."

"By the way," Adriano asked, "what was the pope's reaction to your advisory to cancel church services next month in honor of National Religious Equality Day?"

"He's conferring with his cardinals and advisers. I think it will go through, just in time to keep people out of church the Sunday before Christmas when Christian believers will be wanting it most," Vittorio suppressed a chuckle.

"The Jews and Muslims can't argue with that," Adriano replied.

Vittorio said, "Surprisingly, some of their leaders have protested in fear that they, too, could be prohibited from worship for one of their religious holidays in the future."

Adriano replied, "I assume you reassured them."

Vittorio snorted, "Like all good politicians, I tickled their ears with what they wanted to hear."

It was Adriano's turn to laugh. "Nice work, Vittorio—I mean, President Russo."

"Please, Adriano, you can call me Vittorio when others are not around. We have worked together for a long time. It is right to acknowledge our partnership as we prepare to embrace victory together!" Sipping from a bottle of Perrier water, Vittorio continued, "The economic storm will hit by the end of the year. Chaos will follow into the new year and throw the world economic forum into panic as it struggles to upright the sinking ship following the global market crash. With the plan you and I are devising, I'll be a shoo-in to save the day."

"With me as second-in-command?" Adriano could not resist asking.

"Of course, my devoted associate. The next agenda item after I am confirmed as world leader will be the Middle East peace agreement, which will last, oh, just about three and a half years."

"Then kaboom!" Adriano responded enthusiastically.

"That's right. It all breaks loose around the planet, and my position as world ruler will be permanently established. All these years, these millennia, of planning will finally be fulfilled."

*****

"Hey," Nicholas said as he clicked to answer his cell phone. He was surprised to see Amy was calling him. He had not heard anything from her since she decided to break off their friendship in late

October. "How are you?" Something told him she was not doing well.

He was right.

"Nicholas, I am so sorry for dropping you suddenly last month." Her voice sounded teary. "Quentin came on to me, and for some reason, I fell for it. I don't even know why except that he's a football player, and I wasn't sure if I was ready for the direction my friendship with you was heading." She stopped to swallow a sob.

"It's okay, Amy, really. We all have different preferences and comfort levels. Coach asked about you last week, and I told him we weren't seeing each other much anymore now that my biology grades have improved."

His half-humorous tone drew a slight giggle from Amy. "I hope the tutoring did help. You were doing well in your other classes. You just needed a little nudge with biology."

"And you supplied that beautifully," Nicholas said warmly to reassure her, and it was true. "But how are you? Are classes going okay?" He repressed his inclination to ask about Quentin.

"Sure, they're fine. I got through midterms. How about you?"

"Yep, with a few sleepless nights and more coffee than I should be drinking, I got the grades I wanted."

"That's wonderful, Nicholas. The semester break will be here before we know it." There was a slightly uncomfortable pause before she added, "I-I'm not seeing Quentin anymore. I had to break it off. He didn't...respect me the way you did." She paused again.

"I see," Nicholas said, trying to hide his joy.

"I was wondering if maybe I could go with you to the next Christian students' meeting."

Surprised, he said, "That would be great. The next meeting is Tuesday night before Thanksgiving in Sorren Hall. Will that work with your schedule?"

"I'll make it work," she said thoughtfully. "I want to go."

"All right, I'll save a seat for you."

"Thanks, Nicholas, for being a good...friend."

"You make it easy," he said.

As they said goodbye, he pondered what Amy had told him, and he sensed her vulnerability. *Dear Lord, please heal Amy's hurt and bring her close to you.*

*****

"Honey, don't cry. We'll be fine," Philip said with his arm around Linda's shoulders as they sat together on the family room sofa.

"But I won't get another paycheck for at least a couple of weeks, and I could end up losing this job," she wept.

Philip pulled her head to his shoulder and, keeping his arm around her, took her right hand in his left. "Let's pray."

Linda stilled her sobs and wiped her hands with the tissue in her free hand before closing her eyes.

"Heavenly Father," Philip prayed, "we come before you with heavy hearts but uplifted souls. This world is growing darker each day, but we know that you are the Lord of light and goodness, and you provide for those that love you."

"Yes, Lord, 'Oh, how great *is* your goodness, which you have laid up for those who fear you,'" Linda quoted Psalm 31:19.

"Father God, we acknowledge our sins before you, and we repent of them. Strengthen us with courage and wisdom to live according to your laws and to honor you each day, whatever our circumstances. Thank you for enabling Linda to offer spiritual comfort to Mr. Lyons on his deathbed. We have followed man-made rules and submitted to government authorities as your Word teaches. Your salvation hope triumphs over human restrictions, and we are grateful that Mr. Lyons was able to embrace that hope before taking his last breath on earth."

"Oh yes, Father," Linda chimed in.

"Now, dear Lord, please help us to be wise in managing our finances so we can pay bills on time and meet our daily needs. More than ever, teach us to be frugal and to value every gift you bestow on us each day."

"Yes, God," Linda murmured.

The prayer continued for the couple's children: for Nicholas to continue growing in and be nurtured by his Christian faith, for

Marie to wholeheartedly embrace Christianity and be saved, for Ricky to repent and accept Jesus's atoning death on the cross. The couple prayed that their fragmented family might be reunited whole again in God's kingdom one day.

"Amen," Phil said humbly.

"Amen," Linda echoed.

They hugged each other warmly against the worries that tried to disrupt their calm peace.

"Ready to take a look at revising our budget?" Phil asked.

"Let's get started. I'll make some decaf tea," Linda replied as they stood up, reinforced by their faith, their prayer, and their trust in God's providence.

"You know," Phil said as they headed toward the kitchen table where they would spread out their budget notebook and receipts while sipping tea, "I've never felt closer to God than I do now. And I sense a special bond with Jesus. Do you feel it?"

"I think so," Linda said as she opened the tea canister and turned the stove on under the kettle. "It seems like life is getting harder each day, but Jesus's presence feels near. Do you think the rapture is going to happen soon?"

"I sure hope so," Phil said as he organized the papers on the table.

The following Sunday morning, Reverend Skinner walked up the three steps to the platform pulpit and faced his congregation with a grave expression.

"My beloved brothers and sisters in Christ, welcome this morning as we join to worship our holy God, the everlasting Prince of peace."

Several echoes of "amen" rang through the congregation.

"But our Creator and Redeemer are so much more than that. I cannot begin to describe the many names by which he has made himself known to generations of the faithful. But that will be another message if, Lord willing, we remain here many days in the future."

A buzz circulated through the pews as people wondered what the pastor's words meant.

"As you all know, I monitor the world news to understand how the world is changing and the role of our church in it. In my nearly half century of life, I have never seen or heard the widely published things in news media today. In Luke 17:26, it is recorded that Jesus prophesied, 'And as it was in the days of Noah, so it will be also in the days of the Son of Man.'"

Murmurs of agreement could be heard.

Reverend Skinner continued, "In Luke 17:28–30, Jesus gives a clear visual reminder of what the world will look like when he returns.

"'*Likewise as it was also in the days of Lot: They ate, they drank, they bought, they sold, they planted, they built; but on the day that Lot went out of Sodom it rained fire and brimstone from heaven and destroyed them all. Even so will it be in the day when the Son of Man is revealed.*' Does it seem to you that the world today is like it was in the time of Noah?"

"Yes!"

"For sure!"

"Certainly!"

Everyone agreed.

"And we have heard the horror stories of Sodom and Gomorrah, how no one and nothing was sacred, how innocents were offered to perverts to appease their blood lust. Does that sound anything like our culture today?"

Several comments resounded around the sanctuary, affirming the similarities.

"Church family, it is not just American society that has become corrupt and defiled. The world is under the control of Satan and his demons. Even worse is the fact that people are blinded to their sins and filthy deeds. Isaiah prophesied in chapter 5 verse 20: 'Woe to those who call evil good, and good evil; Who put darkness for light, and light for darkness; Who put bitter for sweet, and sweet for bitter!' Brothers and sisters, our world has been turned upside down. Sadly, most people don't even notice. Or if they do, they don't care. Innocents are being destroyed in the womb, in their homes, and on their beds. Human life is not considered precious. God is not viewed as holy. Evil has usurped God's throne and drunkenly rules over the hearts and lives of men and women today in our culture and around the world."

Silence reigned as everyone listened intently.

Nicholas sat, head bowed, processing every word. He had seen how bad the world was becoming, but the pastor, with the Bible's help, made the message clear and compelling.

Philip's arm rested on the pew around Linda's shoulders and tightened briefly as the reverend paused. Glancing around, he half hoped and half dreaded seeing Jackal in the back, but he was not there.

"Fellow believers in Christ," Reverend Skinner resumed, "there is no time to waste. Global events are shaping up at an alarming rate. Damascus is almost destroyed. The Arab nations are considering peace treaties with Israel. Iran, Russia, and Turkey form the unholy alliance that will bear down on the Holy Land in the prophetic future. All these events were foretold in the Old Testament and the New Testament. We have studied them. Now they are being fulfilled before our eyes if we bother to look!"

His glance swept the wide room to encompass everyone there.

"Don't be taken in by Satan's deceptions. Our time grows short. He knows this, and he prowls around like a fierce lion to destroy anyone in his path. Get out of the way, stay back! Don't give in to the lures of this world, the lust of the eyes, and the pride of life!"

The reverend paused again. "I don't pretend to know the date of Jesus's return, but it is imminent! Maybe this minute, the next hour, today, a month from now, another year. But he is coming soon to rapture believers out of this world and into his kingdom."

Clapping and cheers went up immediately and lasted several seconds.

Reverend Skinner lowered his voice and said, "Don't you feel it—Jesus's presence? The Holy Spirit is among us. He lives in the heart of every believer. Jesus is coming near, just like the first time in Bethlehem over two thousand years ago."

Phil felt goosebumps running up his arms and across his neck. Linda had felt it too. She reached for his hand, and they both turned to Nicholas and exchanged smiles.

A loud voice seldom heard proclaimed from the back-center pew. An elderly man stood up and braced himself on the pew's back before him. "He's coming! The trump will sound soon! He's almost here!"

Awed by the unexpected awakening of old Vernon Jeffers, the congregation laughed joyfully and clapped their hands as they murmured in excitement.

"Go in peace," Reverend Skinner smiled, lifting his hands in benediction over the congregation. "And be ready, Jesus is coming very soon. You could meet him face-to-face at any moment!"

"Amen!" Vernon Jeffers shouted as he shuffled toward the back exit to the church lobby.

*****

"I don't know," Marie said to Bob as he switched off the television that evening. "There's something about Truth Temple that makes me uncomfortable. What about you?"

"Seems okay," Bob said, stifling a yawn. "What are we taking to your parents for Thanksgiving dinner this year?"

"Pecan pie and sweet potato casserole," she said absentmindedly. "Mel said something about the adult Bible study group going to La Grille next week. They serve liquor there, which I'm okay with, but I thought church people avoided places like that. Plus, someone told me they have 'dancers,' not 'dancing,' there one night a week."

"Nothing wrong with that," Bob said, checking the sports scores on his phone.

Marie continued, "Yesterday, Desiree invited me to join a couples' website called Torch. I'm not sure exactly what it's about, but it almost seemed like a swingers' club."

"You mean like marriage swingers?" Bob asked, glancing from his phone.

"I guess. But I kind of doubt Desiree would be on something like that. And if she is, why would she invite me to join when she hardly knows us?"

"It's probably a pyramid scheme or something where she earns points or gets rewards for recruiting new members," Bob said, returning to his phone.

"Seems fishy to me," Marie said. "It sure is a different feeling than when I used to go to church with my parents and brothers."

"That was at least four or five years ago, right? Times have changed. Loosen up those high and mighty morals, or you won't have any friends," Bob suggested, getting up and heading for the kitchen. "I'm having a snack before bed. Want something?"

"No, thanks," Marie said. She sat there, trying to put together the few pieces of a vague puzzle she had collected so far, but they were not adding up. Well, she and Bob could stop attending that church anytime, although she didn't want to hurt Desiree and Mel's feelings.

Her phone buzzed to announce a text message. "Hey, girl," Desiree had written, "post a pic on Torch, okay? You'll meet more members that way."

Not interested, Marie thought. But then a thought struck her. Maybe she should put up a picture to see what happened. She had never done much with social media, but it would be interesting to see who might comment on her profile. She found a picture in the photo area of her phone and uploaded it to the site.

*****

"Hey, Ricky, wake up, man. I said wake up," Jackal prompted, nudging the passed-out youth on the floor with his foot. Ricky didn't budge. Grinning, Jackal muttered, "That right, just stay there."

*****

"Another Sunday night, and I'm ready for bed early again," Phil said as he raised his arms in a stretch. "Are you doing okay? Do you want me to take a half-day off work to be with you?"

"No, honey, I'll be fine. It'll be strange not going to work, but I'll try to look at it as a long-overdue vacation."

"Smart," Phil said, walking over to kiss her cheek. "See you upstairs. I love you."

"Love you too," Linda grinned, feeling relieved now that she and Philip had turned their crisis over to the Lord and were taking active steps to address it.

The evening air seemed crisp and expectant. There was the sense that something significant was going to happen. The weight of the previous troubles seemed to become lighter. The feeling was hopeful.

As he headed for the steps, the doorbell rang. Phil exchanged a surprised glance with Linda. "Who's that?"

"I don't know," she said. "Maybe Reverend Skinner? Or Ricky?"

Phil walked through the family room to the foyer and looked through the narrow side window panel beside the door. Unbolting the lock, he opened the door and said, "Good evening, how can—"

Just then, a trumpet sounded, and a bright light appeared. For those in Christ, it was the moment they looked forward to for many years. Jesus was taking his children from this wicked world, and it was exciting.

At once, he disappeared into thin air. Startled, the youth with gun raised and aimed where Philip had stood turned quickly to find Linda, but she was also mysteriously gone!

The gun went off as Jackal's trigger finger nervously pressed it unthinkingly. Dressed in black clothing and a balaclava hood, Jackal called, "Nicholas! I know you're here. Your car's in the driveway." Jackal dashed up the steps to check the bedrooms. Finding the one belonging to Ricky's younger brother, he pushed the half-open door and heard upbeat music from the cell phone playlist. He saw a desk light shining on an open textbook beside a laptop computer that showed some kind of college assignment on the monitor. An empty chair faced the computer.

The hair on the back of Jackal's neck stood up. What had happened? Was it a mirage, a trick? Shaking his head, he wondered if he was having a delayed reaction to the drugs he had used yesterday.

Taking the steps leading downstairs two at a time, Jackal paused in the foyer for a closer look at where the Bullocks had been standing and looked around to see if they were hiding somewhere. The house was eerily quiet and empty. He darted through the front door and disappeared into the darkness.

CHAPTER 12

In the swirling mist, four people stayed close together as they moved forward in small steps. Uncertain and somewhat fearful, they could not see more than a few feet ahead, but they heard a low hum of voices in the distance.

In the twinkling of an eye, they had been caught up in the spirit of Jesus Christ, Lord and Savior, in the clouds where no human eye could see them. Joining thousands of others, they caught glimpses of long-deceased loved ones as well as current church members and friends. The excitement of being with Jesus overshadowed everything else. A moment later, they found themselves standing in the mist and just able to recognize those in their group without seeing further beyond. Content to know they had arrived in God's kingdom, they did not know what would happen next. It was both unsettling and exciting.

Philip Bullock reached for the hand of the person beside him and received a quick squeeze. The faint voices in the distance grew more distinct; they were approaching. It sounded like a vast multitude!

"Linda, we made it! Nicholas, are you all right?"

"Yes, I'm fine! Glory to God in the highest!"

"Amen" and "amen" were echoed by Philip and Linda, along with a fourth person on the other side of Nicholas.

"Marie?" Philip asked, trying not to tremble with the hope that his daughter had been caught up in the rapture with them.

"Amy," a small, unsure voice said.

Shocked, Phil and Marie glanced at the girl that Nicholas had casually told them about.

"Are we...still a family now?" Nicholas asked Linda.

"I think so," Phil said, "but not in the same way as we were on earth. We're now part of a much bigger family, the believers in God who accepted Jesus's atoning death for their sins and gave up the world to follow him."

Just as he was about to reassure everyone that there was no need to be afraid, the thick mist began to part in a swirling haze that divided before the group as a blinding shaft of light pierced through. The light grew brighter and more intense than anything they had seen before, like a nuclear explosion. It was stunning and spectacular!

Immobile, the man stood resolute to face what was coming, holding on to faith.

As voices approached, the Bullock family recognized the sounds of loved ones that had preceded them in death. Clusters of people embraced the newly arrived family members with joy and laughter. It was like a huge family reunion with people of every race, ethnicity, and complexion that had lived on earth surrounding the new arrivals.

Everyone walked together through a beautiful garden archway adorned by fruitful branches and scented blossoms. Birds of various species sang all around them in the trees and hedges, and domestic animals romped through the lush garden and across fields of blooming flowers. Amid the garden stood the majestic tree of life with branches swaying in a gentle breeze. The celestial city lay just ahead, its white walls gleaming with enormous gates, revealing studded jewels and gold trim. Everyone was oohing and aahing as they drew closer, amazed by the sights they had read about in the Bible but could never have imagined as being so gorgeous and awe-inspiring.

Tall, powerfully built angels of a dazzling white appearance stood at various points along the path to guide the new arrivals into the city of heaven.

The judgment hall stood before the crowd, impassive and imposing. One by one, names were called by mighty angels, one on each side of the massive entrance. Each person was to enter—unaccompanied and unencumbered with earthly goods that had been left behind—to walk the wide corridor illuminated by the glory of God that filled the place instead of artificial or natural light. Scented censers released fragrant odors of burning incense to honor the Lord as described in the book of Revelation.

Philip Bullock went first, moving down the corridor toward the massive judgment seat of Christ. As he approached, he saw numerous angels attending on the Lord of hosts who sat on the throne of judgment. The angels stood on both sides of the throne platform and spoke words of welcome to Philip. Six humans sat on either side of the Lord who Philip believed must be the disciples. He saw others seated nearby and assumed that the apostle Paul and reverent followers, like Timothy, Titus, and others, were among that group. Trembling inside as he tried to grasp the reality of his location, Philip struggled to hold on to his courage. He wasn't afraid of being condemned because he had accepted Jesus as Savior, and he knew his sins were forgiven. Instead, he was humbled to find himself among this august group of epic Christian leaders and God himself. Reaching the judgment seat, he could not lift his eyes to see the face of the Almighty. Instead, he bowed down, prostrate on the ground before the King of the universe.

"My Savior and my God," he murmured, trying not to tremble as the angels lifted their voices in musical praise and worship. A form approached and stood beside him. Looking up, Philip was overjoyed to meet Jesus face-to-face. Tears filled Philip's eyes as Jesus smiled gently, glory filling his face.

The angel Gabriel, standing on the right side of the throne, stepped forward and opened a large volume on a table, which Philip knew to be the Book of Life. As he began to read, the angel recited key events of Philip's life, starting in childhood and continuing up to the moment of the rapture, which had seemed a mere fraction of a second.

As many long-forgotten deeds were mentioned, Philip felt deep shame and regret creep over him. Tears formed in the corners of his eyes and began to trickle down his cheeks as he lay on the ground, facing the floor. How could God forgive all his wrongs? Why was he standing in the presence of the Creator of the universe, the Savior of all humankind? He did not deserve it. He deserved to be banished to the pit of hell. He knew it, and God knew it.

But the angel Gabriel was saying more. "Despite your wrong-doing in life, Philip Bullock, you accepted Jesus Christ as your Savior and allowed his death on the cross to pay for your sins."

Just then, Jesus, in full shining brilliance, stepped up beside Philip. Helping the man to his feet, Jesus shone in his Shechinah glory that left Philip speechless.

A booming voice that sounded like heavy thunder over a cascading waterfall called out: "Jesus, my Son, you offer your sacrifice of earthly death to pay for the sins of Philip Bullock."

"Yes, Father." Jesus stood still and calm as Philip waited in trepidation for judgment to be pronounced. He knew he had been saved, but what if he had misunderstood?

"Philip, your sins are absolved. Welcome to our eternal kingdom."

Smiling and choked up with emotion, Philip felt Jesus's arms around his shoulders in a firm hug. This was the moment he had longed for since a child. Now he could rest easy, knowing that his salvation was confirmed for eternity. Hopefully, the same would be true for his loved ones and for all who entered the gates of heaven.

"My name is Malachi. Come," another tall angel said, taking his arm and leading him out of the judgment hall to a street of lovely white dwelling places that reflected divine glory. "Your place is over there, the second one from the end."

"It's beautiful," Philip breathed in awe. Indeed, it was made of white stone like the others, and the design included strategically placed windows for light. Mosses and springtime flowers grew around the side of the house. It was both stately and straightforward in a style that far surpassed any on earth.

Inside, the home was comfortably furnished with living utensils and furniture. Open, airy, and spacious—it was a perfect dream home.

Turning, he thanked the angel who inclined his head to acknowledge gratitude before returning to the judgment hall. As he left, another angel, whose name was Mattan, was escorting Linda who looked eagerly around everywhere to catch every sight she could. When she saw Philip standing in the doorway, she glanced at the angel with her, who nodded, and rushed over to the man who had been her earthly husband. Here in heaven, their relationship was far more than that, and the physical component was no longer needed, surpassed by the pervasive love that streamed through the air among all who now resided here.

"Philip, we made it!" she said happily. "I can't believe it. This is a dream come true!"

"Wait until you see the house," he said. "You'll love it."

Eagerly, he led the way inside as she said, "Nicholas was after me. He should be joining us shortly."

"And Amy?" Philip asked.

"I don't know. I had not met her before or talked to her since she and Nicholas started seeing each other again."

"I can't imagine anyone being allowed through the gates of heaven who would not be allowed to stay."

"But there will be the great white throne judgment," Philip reminded Linda.

"Will it take place here or elsewhere?" Linda asked as she began looking around inside the house.

"I thought it would be in heaven. I guess we will find out eventually," Philip mused.

Moments later, Nicholas entered their new home, and the three family members embraced.

"I'm so glad we are here together," Linda said. "Have you seen Ricky? Was he raptured too?"

"He wasn't in the crowd that I could see," Philip said.

"What about Marie?" Linda asked sadly.

"I didn't see her. Did you, Nicholas?" Philip asked.

"No."

They were quiet, reflecting on what this meant.

"They can still make it," Linda said, cheering up. "Marie knows what to do."

"Ricky does too, but that didn't help him up to now," Philip said.

"Let's hope they can make it through the tribulation," Linda said hopefully.

"God will give them every chance," Philip said.

"Amen," Nicholas agreed. Glancing down the road, he saw Amy with another angel and waved. She waved back happily. It was good seeing the peace in her face as the angel led her to another dwelling around the corner.

"It's so good to be here," he said.

"A dream come true," Linda murmured. "Look, here comes Reverend Skinner."

Another angel led the pastor down the road past their dwelling to the one at the end, next to a beautiful garden of what appeared to be wildflowers.

"Hello, neighbors," he called cheerfully.

"Hi, Reverend Skinner!" Philip called.

"Welcome to the neighborhood," Linda added as Nicholas grinned.

As the angel explained the house to the reverend, they turned to see another new arrival, Gloria Skinner, being led by a friendly-looking angel who was listening as she talked excitedly about the new mansion.

"Hey there!" she called to the Bullocks while passing their house.

"Good seeing you on this side of eternity," Linda said cheerfully. "Neighbors forever!"

"Amen to that," Gloria said before resuming her questions to the angel about the house she would be inhabiting.

A short time later, everyone met in the quiet road. "Let's gather with the worshippers at the throne of grace," Reverend Skinner said. The Bullocks joined him and Gloria as they headed to the temple of God to give him praise and gratitude. There, they were introduced to the disciples and the apostles at last, filling them with astonishment and excitement as they eagerly joined the worshipping throng of believers at the throne of God.

"So much joy is unbelievable," Linda said during a pause. "Did you ever think we would find ourselves so richly blessed?"

"Not to this degree," Philip said. "I appreciated God's goodness on earth. But here, it is everywhere. We can feel it all the time!" He paused before adding, "It's unfortunate that those left behind must now go through the tribulation, but it was their choice. Let us hope they change their minds and come to join the believers here."

"It won't be easy," Nicholas said tentatively.

"No, but it will be worth it once they make up their minds to accept Jesus as the only way to heaven."

"I am delighted to be here," Philip said, turning his eyes and heart again to the God of heaven and earth and bowing low before the Creator and their Savior as the others followed suit.

Legions of angelic voices filled the air with music and praise as the scent of incense rose above all, like a blessing to be diffused among the worshippers.

The archangel Gabriel stepped forward and stated in a loud voice: "Blessed is the Lord God Almighty who is, who was, and who is to come!"

Thousands of voices rose in a resounding cheer.

"Saints of the world, you have been accepted into the kingdom of God because you placed your faith in the death of God's only Son on the cross at Jerusalem over two thousand years ago. More saints are coming in the future, but many other people chose to follow Satan. The fulfillment of their destiny will be pronounced at the great white throne judgment that is to come."

Concerned murmurs and low talking ensued as Gabriel stopped speaking. He paused to let this information be absorbed before continuing, "Many of you have studied the Bible and know the order of events. But others have not had that privilege. Here, then, is God's timeline for the next actions in his great plan for humankind." The archangel opened a scroll and began reading loudly so that his voice resounded throughout the temple. "These are the words of the apostle John from the vision he saw while exiled on the isle of Patmos about what is to come for the unbelievers after their earthly death.

"Revelation 20:11–12, '*And I saw a great white throne, and him that sat on it, from whose face the earth and the heaven fled away; and there was found no place for them. And I saw the dead, small and great, stand before God; and the books were opened: and another book was opened, which is the book of life: and the dead were judged out of those things which were written in the books, according to their works.*'

Revelation 20:13–15, '*And the sea gave up the dead which were in it; and death and hell delivered up the dead which were in them: and they were judged every man according to their works. And death and hell were cast into the lake of fire. This is the second death. And whosoever was not found written in the book of life was cast into the lake of fire.*'"

Weeping could be heard within the throng of believers, along with a few whispers and moans.

Gabriel looked up and said compassionately, "Do not grieve for the lost. They have chosen their way deliberately. All are given the same opportunity to be saved. There is still time. The tribulation spoken of by the prophets is about to begin in a short span of earth years that will seem like days here. God is faithful. He will offer the choice that each of you was given." He paused and looked around. "God himself will wipe the tears from your eyes."

Linda turned to Philip and Nicholas. "I hope Marie and Ricky will make the right choice."

"I do too," Philip said gravely, placing an affectionate hand on Nicholas's shoulder.

*****

"What the—" Ricky rubbed his eyes and sat up in response to the sharp kick that had roused him from a drug-fueled stupor.

"Get up, stupid," Jackal hissed. "Somethin's goin' on."

As he tried to focus his eyes, Ricky could see Jackal's unclear form taking shape before his eyes. He felt terrible, physically and mentally, but that was not unusual. What was strange was Jackal's apparent anger, which he did not usually show mainly because he generally had things under control.

"Wha' happened?" Ricky muttered, his mouth feeling full of cotton.

"I dunno. Something weird is goin' on, probably a trick of some kind. Look outside." He gestured toward the fly-stained window where the worn fiberglass curtains had been pulled back to show a view of the street two stories below at ground level.

Slowly pulling himself up with a hand boost from the sofa, Ricky ambled over to the window and looked outside. There was less traffic than usual for the evening. And even in the darkness, he could see several vehicles sitting in the middle of the road or parked jerkily to the curb. Residents had congregated in groups on the street and were talking animatedly and pointing at the cars and looking up at the sky.

Ricky rubbed his eyes again. "Meteor?" he suggested.

Jackal let forth a string of profanities. "I don't know!" he exploded. "Asteroid, foreign invasion, underground hiding. I don't know what the heck is going on."

Slowly, the thoughts in Ricky's head began to come together. He remembered hearing his parents, along with Pastor Skinner, speak of the end-times and the so-called rapture of Christian believers. But that had been several years ago when he was still a teenager living at home and going to church on Sundays. He had never read much of the Bible, so all his information about the prophecies came second-hand from the spiritual adults in his life back then. He had long ago stopped thinking about Jesus returning to take the saints out of the world and unleashing the full powers of Satan and hell. Recalling those memories, he felt goosebumps prickle on his arms.

"What is this about?" Jackal snarled, hating for his carefully laid plans to be disturbed.

Ricky searched his memory for details but found nothing worth stating. If this was the rapture, he was not going since he had turned his back on God and Jesus long ago.

"No idea, and I couldn't care less. Idiot church people might be able to explain it, but probably none of 'em are around anymore."

Jackal gave him an appraising look. "How do you know? You too strung out all the time to know what's happening."

For the first time in a very long time, Ricky looked Jackal in the eye. "I heard about this stuff when I was a kid. You probably don't have a clue. If it's what I think, they're gone, man. All the Christians were taken out."

"By thugs?" Jackal asked, not understanding.

"By Jesus. The Bible predicted this, and it might be coming true."

"Where'd they go?" Jackal asked, as enthused as a small boy listening to a fairy tale.

Ricky sighed. "To heaven where you're not going, and I'm not going. We're stuck here, and that's fine by me."

Jackal studied Ricky appraisingly as if thinking the youth was still on a drug high. Finally, he said, "You want me to believe all the churchgoers flew up to the skies and left this world?"

"No," Ricky said, losing patience. "Just the Christians, the ones who actually believed in Jesus and became his followers. Not everyone goes to church with the same views."

"I didn't know that," Jackal said thoughtfully. "I thought they all believed the same thing."

"Well, they don't. And many so-called Christians are hypocrite liars, which is why I stopped going to church and believing that. And I'm not looking back. I can take care of myself."

Jackal was not so sure that Ricky could look after himself, given his prolific drug use, but he kept quiet. Maybe he could use Ricky's confidence for his own purposes. Looking out the window again, he felt a cold chill. Something big was up, and he wasn't sure how that would impact his life or society overall.

News reports poured in from countries around the globe. Millions of people had disappeared, and no one knew where they were. Theories suggested they had gone secretly underground or had been abducted by aliens. Others claimed they had abandoned their former lives and taken new identities. Churchgoers that still remained along with some pastors and administrators familiar with Bible doctrine and end-times prophecies understood that the rapture had occurred, and they had been left behind. Many wept and mourned. Others tried to reorganize the remaining congregation members to renew their study of the Scriptures so they could understand how to be saved in the terrible days that would be coming soon after the rapture. On the internet, searches surged for Christian doctrine, messages about God, and prophecies about Jesus. Many people had an idea about what had occurred, but far more had no clue and were badly frightened about what was happening.

The holiday season dragged on because of global uncertainty and near chaos in many countries. Few Christmas decorations were put up, and many churches were no longer meeting even before President Russo's new holiday commemorating All Religion Day that actually meant No Church Day—the Sunday before Christmas—which the pope had endorsed. Global events began to fall quickly into place to form a new world order, which became the priority item on the scheduled December 26 agenda of the global economic reset forum. The group of world leaders now established the goal of electing a calm and experienced leader who could bring peace and order to a world that had spun out of control. As planned, Vittorio Russo was elected as the world director the day after Christmas. The holiday season had been overshadowed by strange events that had left humanity as a whole feeling dejected and afraid. They didn't know what to expect next except that it would probably be something as bad or worse as what had already occurred.

"We will rebuild the world," Director Russo promised in his acceptance speech, "starting with the economy and progressing to social issues to ensure every human being enjoys the same basic rights and freedoms everywhere on the planet. In collaboration with the Israeli government, we will build a new temple, one that they proclaim as the third temple. But for all of us of every faith, it will be a new and lasting place of worship for people of any religious belief."

Russo's speeches and promises were met with enthusiasm and acclaim. Everyone wanted something to believe in and hope for, and Vittorio Russo provided them with security and support.

*****

"Ricky! Where have you been? I've been trying to reach you for days!" Marie almost wept with relief at hearing her brother's voice as he finally answered her call.

"Same as always, nothing new," he sneered. "So you didn't make it either, going aloft or whatever they call it. Should I say 'too bad' or 'good for you'?"

"Don't you care!" she shouted into the phone. "Mom and Dad and Nicholas are gone. Everyone we knew that was a Christian is gone. Now we're stuck here, and everything is ten times worse than it was before. Crime is exploding, kids are offered in sacrifices, companies are shutting down. The economy is doomed!" she said hotly. "We'll never see our family again."

"The economy is going to be revived by the global economic reset director or whatever his title is," Ricky said, surprising himself that he had gleaned this information from the news, which he did not often pay attention to, and that he had remembered it. "No worries." His current hit of dope had relaxed him enough to listen to his sister, or he would not have answered her call.

Marie started crying as she said, "Things will never be the same. The world is coming to an end, and all you can do is...is..." She caught herself from criticizing him. She wanted to be her brother's ally, not his accuser. "Look, let's stay at Mom and Dad's house and figure this out. The assistant pastor at their church didn't make it in the rapture, but he's calling around and trying to get us all back into the Bible to figure out how to survive the tribulation. Join us please!" she begged. "And don't take the mark, the ID tattoo that the new leader introduced in his speech. It'll be coming soon. If you take it, you can never get into heaven."

"You're crazy," Ricky said. "I've already signed up for it to receive the universal basic income. I gotta have it to survive."

"You can't!" Marie said heavily. "Please, Ricky."

"And you know what? There's a bounty on those who don't take it. I'm going to turn in your and Bob's names to get my reward. Gotta go," Ricky said, clicking to end the call.

"What did he say?" Bob asked, coming over to hug Marie who was sobbing.

"He hung up on me, wants no part of Jesus," Marie wept. "He's going to turn us in for not taking the mark. It's going to get worse. We have to get ready for the tribulation and Jesus's second coming."

"We will," Bob said calmly. "I should have taken this seriously when your parents tried talking to us. Truth Temple was just a delusion."

"And a distraction," Marie sniffed. "If we had kept going to church with Mom and Dad, we wouldn't be here now. I wish I'd never posted my picture on that website, although fortunately, nothing happened."

"We'll go back to your parents' church and get ready for what's coming," Bob promised.

*****

Director Russo and his assistant, Adriano Alba, organized the new-world government by influencing world rulers to adopt the global economic system developed and implemented quickly. The new system would be enforced by a tattooed ID number on each person's hand or forehead. Although invisible, some people preferred to have it implanted where it would be less likely to cause temporary redness or swelling so they had the choice of the back of their hand or the left side of their forehead. There would be no more cash or credit cards, just the mark, which would be scanned at every place of business now being outfitted for its use.

Everyone who had been registered during the last census was notified to get the mark on a specific date. It was administered at the city's administration building where long lines of citizens waited their turn for the procedure that took less than ten minutes.

Ricky and Jackal took the mark within a day of each other. It enabled them to operate an illicit drug business that the local government was aware of but allowed to exist anyway. Infused with new power and potential wealth, Ricky reduced his drug use and focused on recruiting new users, or "customers," to build his financial empire. He bought a town house in the luxury section of Philadelphia and soon had a dozen lackeys working for him.

Jackal was thrown off balance by Ricky's rise to power. He spent more time at home, depressed and hungover than ever before.

Encountering his mother in the apartment one morning after being out all night, he saw she was reading the Bible.

"Why you doin' that?" he asked as she sat at the kitchen table.

"Gordon left me, said he had to go back to his wife and kids." She paused as though thinking. "I remember my grandmother reading the Bible whenever trouble came. That's why I am readin' it now. I don't know what to do anymore, but maybe the Holy Book can help."

Brow furrowed, Jackal felt more aftershocks from the rapture event that many were continuing to discuss. He couldn't understand what had happened to the Christians who had suddenly disappeared, but maybe he should try. No one else seemed to have reasonable answers to his questions, and daily life had become more confusing and stressful than ever. After his mother left for her housecleaning job later that day, he sat down at the table and opened the Bible to the New Testament. A pamphlet he'd found lying on the sidewalk had urged readers to look up the book of John. Jackal began reading there.

Those who had been left behind took one of two directions. Many chose to ignore the rapture as an unusual event, like witnessing a UFO, and dismissed it as unimportant. Others were filled with a desire to survive the coming tribulation that they either had heard of or now learned about as they returned to the churches that remained or began reading the Bible to learn what to expect in the future. They wanted to spend eternity with Jesus Christ and God forever in glory, and they avidly studied the Bible and met in small groups, like those of the early church, to discuss what they were reading and to help each other. The days on earth grew darker and more desperate.

Three and a half years later, Director Russo broke the peace agreement he had made with Israel. His troops violated the temple in Jerusalem, replaced holy images with images of the rulers, and then set them on the altar. Everyone who entered the temple had to bow down and worship Russo's image. Those that did not were immediately seized, imprisoned, tried, and executed for treason.

Many who had become believers after the rapture were persecuted, betrayed by the authorities, and killed. Beheading was instituted as a common form of capital punishment because it was fast, convenient, and easy to implement. Certain streets were designated for this punishment and became known as thoroughfares of blood.

Those that hid and were able to survive prayed fervently for the second coming of Jesus. They knew the battle would be fierce and deadly, but they longed to meet the Savior face-to-face and to spend eternity with God.

The unbelievers who rejected opportunities to read Scripture and meet with believers took advantage of the abrupt decline in morals to victimize the ignorant and enrich themselves. They had no problem pretending to worship Director Russo, when required by videoconferencing, in exchange for the freedom to conduct their illegal activities that added to the suffering of many.

EPILOGUE

Friends, if you are wondering how to avoid the coming desolation on this earth brought about by Satan and the demons through the Antichrist who will rise to rule the world after the believers are raptured by Jesus, all you need do is believe in Jesus Christ and accept his death on the cross as payment for your sins.

Jesus was born on this earth over two thousand years ago to a virgin mother, begotten of God. He lived for thirty-three years in Israel, preaching the good news of salvation to those who, then and now, confess and repent their sins and follow him. Jesus was falsely convicted of blasphemy by Jewish leaders and died on the cross for the sins of the world. Three days later, he rose from the grave to reveal mastery over death. Forty days later, he ascended into the clouds and is seated at the right hand of God.

All you have to do is believe in Jesus and accept the atonement of his death for your sins personally. Then follow him by praying faithfully, reading the Bible, and meeting with other Christians in a Bible-teaching church or group. There is nothing more you can do to be saved, Only God can save you when you accept Jesus as your Savior.

> *For by grace you have been saved through*
> *faith, and that not of yourselves; it is the gift of God.*
> (Ephesians 2:8 NKJV)

The end-times seem to be upon us, and prophecies are being fulfilled at an astonishing rate. Christian believers around the world will soon be caught up in the air by the Lord Jesus in the twinkle of an eye. The Holy Spirit, who restrains evil to some extent now, will also depart.

The Antichrist will arise to become the ruler of this world and impose a new global commerce system. It will require a bodily mark that all must take to do business, but if you take the mark, you cannot be saved by Jesus. If you do not take it, you will be unable to do business here on earth and will likely be imprisoned or killed.

But have hope, Jesus is coming again to fight Satan and to free believers.

> *Behold, He is coming with clouds, and every eye will see Him, even they who pierced Him. And all the tribes of the earth will mourn because of Him. Even so, Amen.*
>
> *"I am the Alpha and the Omega, the Beginning and the End," says the Lord, "who is and who was and who is to come, the Almighty."* (Revelation 1:7–8 NKJV)

Choose today whom you will serve. You do not have to fear death or worry that you will never see a deceased loved one again. Those who are Christians will be reunited in God's kingdom. It is not too late to accept Jesus as your Savior and be forgiven of every sin you ever committed. The moment you die, you will be escorted to heaven by angels. If Jesus returns before that for his followers, you will be raptured from this world with the other believers as explained by the apostle Paul.

> *Behold, I tell you a mystery: We shall not all sleep, but we shall all be changed—in a moment, in the twinkling of an eye, at the last trumpet. For the trumpet will sound, and the dead will be raised incorruptible, and we shall be changed. For this corruptible must put on incorruption, and this mortal must put on immortality.* (1 Corinthians 15: 51–53 NKJV)

The unbelievers that remain on the earth will be deluded by Satan to accept the rule of a seeming man of peace, who is the Antichrist. A terrible tribulation period will be followed by a great war in which evildoers will be defeated. Satan will be bound for one thousand years then released, and he will organize the final battle against God and the saints. He will be again defeated. The great white throne judgment will bring forth all that have died for final, permanent judgment—the lake of fire for sinners and a new heaven and earth for Christians.

> *Now I saw a new heaven and a new earth, for the first heaven and the first earth had passed away. Also, there was no more sea. Then I, John, saw the holy city, New Jerusalem, coming down out of heaven from God, prepared as a bride adorned for her husband. And I heard a loud voice from heaven saying, "Behold, the tabernacle of God is with men, and He will dwell with them, and they shall be His people. God Himself will be with them and be their God."* (Revelation 21:1–3 NKJV)

Do not wait to be saved! Call on the name of the Lord Jesus Christ right now, repent of your sins, and accept him as your Savior. Then you too will hear the trumpet call of the Lord when he removes the Christian believers from this world before the tribulation begins. The prophecies are being fulfilled to reveal the end-time predictions outlined in the Bible. Do not ignore the warning signs! Seek God while he may be found before it is too late. God loves you and wants you to be saved, but he leaves the decision to you.

Prayer: *Dear God, please forgive me, for I have broken your laws and sinned against you. Accept me into your kingdom and help me to become a dedicated follower. In Jesus's name, I pray this. Amen.*

ABOUT THE AUTHOR

Bishop Eric A. Lambert Jr. is the senior pastor of the Bethel Deliverance International Church. Bishop Lambert also serves as the presiding bishop of the Bethel Deliverance International Fellowship of Churches. The goal of the organization is to train pastors and ministers in the work of ministry and promote unity among the churches worldwide.

A man of vision, recognizing that media communication is a key thread to the expansion of the kingdom of God, Bishop Lambert seeks to proclaim the glorious gospel of Jesus Christ through several media outlets. Bishop Lambert desires that Christ be proclaimed throughout the world. Through the daily and weekly television broadcast, *Climbing Higher*, many souls are won to the kingdom of God. Realizing that the call of God would take him to foreign nations, Bishop Lambert began to study foreign languages. He speaks fluent Italian and proficient Russian.

Bishop Lambert completed studies at various fine Christian institutions. Bishop Lambert has earned his bachelor's degree in psychology from Liberty University and earned his master's degree in forensic psychology from Nova Southeastern University of Fort Lauderdale, Florida. A noted author and prolific writer, Bishop Lambert is the author of many other books. Among the titles are *The Kneeling Mind*, *The Christian and the Culture*, *At What Cost*, and *Cancel the Culture*. Bishop Lambert is married to Lady Sheila Lambert, and they are the proud parents of Shaneena and the godparents of Darius.